Spiritual Warfare and the Armor of God is a clarion call to every Christ follower. It is time for the church to wake up and strap on the full armor of God because the enemy's weapons are trained against us and the warfare is great. Luanne Botta has written a wise and practical book that teaches us to not only be prepared for the battle against us, but to go into it fully prepared and stronger than our enemy.

—*Donna VanLiere*
New York Times bestselling author and teacher

Luanne Botta was an ordained instructor at the Greater Works Bible College for over seven years, training hundreds of students. This book is a must read for all Christians. We need this teaching now more than ever!

—*Rev. Andrew Mitrik*
Dean, Greater Works Bible College, Monroeville, PA

We live in tumultuous times; everyone can sense it. No matter the time or circumstances, God is in complete control and has made preparation for each moment within His created order. This preparation brings biblical revelation, as do His vessels who teach it and execute it. Luanne is one of these vessels who has been prepared for this very hour. This book is not theoretical nor does it simply contain knowledge about *Spiritual Warfare and the Armor of God*. This book contains wisdom and spiritual insight that has been forged in Luanne's life by the Holy Spirit! She lives this every day. This topic and this book have been prepared for "such a moment as this."

—*Richard Nugara, Ph.D.*

Adjunct professor of biblical studies

Regent University

As a former student of Luanne Botta, I am grateful that she immersed us in the Word of God. She taught us the importance of understanding the elements of spiritual warfare and how to combat the enemy with the armor of God. Now, as a kindergarten teacher, I find myself educating and teaching the same things to even the youngest of students. Putting on the armor of God is not something I do for only me, but for every student who walks through my classroom. In the pages of this book, you will find the power, strength, and authority God has rightly given us and commanded us to use through the powerful name of Jesus. Luanne brings insightful truths, wisdom, and clarity into an area we all need to be empowered for our daily lives.

—*Rachel Sadd*

Mother of four; K5 kindergarten teacher

Once again, Luanne has written a powerful word for anyone who has chosen to walk with Jesus. She reminds us of the importance of leaning on the objective standard that is God's truth, as well as the importance of utilizing the full armor of God. This book is a strong reminder that we have an extension of God's power through His armor, but it's up to us to learn how to use what's already been given to us to fight the inevitable battles we face as believers living in a fallen world.

—*Stephanie Baker*
Executive director, Life in Abundance, Greenville, SC

Although I haven't known Luanne Botta for long, I've grown deeply close to her through praying together. She has encouraged me and prayed for me even when I felt too weak to do it for myself. I am eternally grateful for my friend who practices what is in this book by going to battle for those she loves.

—*Kim Harrell*
Missions and outreach director; pastor's wife
New Covenant Church, Greenwood, SC

"For such a time as this." Never has there been a better time in history to take our stand as Christians and equip ourselves with the armor of God. This book is so timely and relevant to Christians everywhere as we must stand on the truth of God's Word in order to battle the enemy's plan to kill, steal, and destroy during this hour. I learned about the armor of God under Luanne Botta's teaching over twenty years ago and still, to this day, recite it and have taught my children to do the same. It has meant everything to me knowing that I can send my kids out into this world feeling confident that they are fully equipped with the armor of God.

—*Cassandra Rockinson*
A warrior parent

SPIRITUAL WARFARE
AND THE
ARMOR OF GOD

THE BATTLE IS REAL…
THE VICTORY IS SURE

LUANNE BOTTA

WHITAKER
HOUSE

SPIRITUAL WARFARE AND THE ARMOR OF GOD
The Battle Is Real…The Victory Is Sure

Guarded Heart Ministries
P.O. Box 50953
Greenwood, SC 29649
www.luannebotta.com

ISBN: 978-1-64123-788-8
eBook ISBN: 978-1-64123-789-5
Printed in the United States of America
© 2021 by Luanne Botta

Edited by Vicki Mlinar

Whitaker House
1030 Hunt Valley Circle
New Kensington, PA 15068
www.whitakerhouse.com

Library of Congress Cataloging-in-Publication Data (Pending)

1 2 3 4 5 6 7 8 9 10 11 ᵾ 28 27 26 25 24 23 22 21

DEDICATION

This book is dedicated to my nieces and nephews.
Stand firm...run your race well!
I love you so!

*Focus on this one thing: Forgetting the past and looking
forward to what lies ahead...press on to reach the end
of the race and receive the heavenly prize for which God,
through Christ Jesus, is calling [you].*
—Philippians 3:13–14 NLT

CONTENTS

FOREWORD

I am a soldier, I fight where I am told,
and I win where I fight.
—Gen. George S. Patton

This bold, confident statement was spoken by "America's fightingest general," who inspired his troops to become a great part in the making of world history.

The timing of this book is God ordained as the world and our country are under siege! At the same time, we may face personal battles that can be long, intense, and exhausting. I will choose to fight alongside this author, who has knowledge of a different warfare. With Christ confidence and a holy boldness, Luanne Botta equips her readers to win where they fight!

In *Spiritual Warfare and the Armor of God*, Luanne shares that we are like soldiers in a war against an enemy fiercer than flesh and blood. Through scriptural strategies and equipment designed in the heavenly realm, she exposes our camouflaged foe and imparts the biblical response for pushback and victory.

Her training has been hard fought through her own personal experiences. Luanne's most definitive training ground was from a high school Bible class. An unusual mentor, this calling and seventeen-year teaching assignment gave Luanne insight and experience from which to draw much of her instruction on the battlefield of life. She is equipping the generations. A full-gospel believer, Luanne's rich biblical understanding is coupled with an anointed prophetic gift. She has heard the Lord as He has co-authored the pages of this battle plan.

Luanne and I are sisters in Christ and sisters through blood. To know her is to discover a beautiful, fun, personable, and faith-filled woman who can befriend a stranger in record time. She loves life, sports, worship music on her car radio, and snuggling with her nieces and nephews. She's one of those warrior princesses who carries her sword at all times. Her heart is one of gold. As siblings, we have shared many years of the joys and disappointments of life, the successes and failures of human experiences and the faith to see us through. Now I share her battle cry: Armor up!

Fierce with the things of darkness, Luanne's discernment is sharp. She senses an urgency as she is emboldened to train you to crush an already defeated foe. I believe the enemy cowers that you hold this book in your hands!

—*Linda Hart*
Assistant to senior pastor, Greater Works Outreach
Monroeville, PA

INTRODUCTION

Submit therefore to God. But resist the devil,
and he will flee from you. Come close to God and He
will come close to you.
—James 4:7–8

I have always been a competitor. I played sports as a kid, and I loved a challenge and loved the satisfaction of winning, even if it came down to the last second. To this day, I love watching my nieces and nephews play sports, cheering them on from the stands. And I am an avid college football fan. I don't care who is playing; I just love the competition and how almost every big game comes down to the final whistle.

I am grateful for those years of competition as it showed me how to respond in life. There are joys when you excel at something you worked so hard at and you grow in strength to handle the drudge of disappointment and defeat. However, when I became a Christian at twenty-two years of age, I realized I had entered a game I was very unfamiliar with. I couldn't see this invisible battle that seemed to be raging over my life. When we accept Jesus Christ as our Lord and Savior, we come into an unseen war. I wasn't aware of that battle until a few years into my walk with Jesus.

Looking back now and seeing the onslaught that came against me in my twenties, I see how the enemy of my soul was trying to prevent me from the ministry that the Lord would be calling me to in just a few more years. Those early years in my twenties were filled with voices of negativity, discouragement, unworthiness, insecurity, paranoia, fear, unhealthy relationships, and so many other things. We may think that is something that is normal as we are maturing and finding our way in life, but this was an onslaught that wasn't close to being normal. I didn't know what I was wrestling with in this unseen world.

In my mid-twenties, I had begun to attend a full gospel church whose main message was that of faith and spiritual warfare. That is where I found the truth of the battle that had been raging over my life and came to realize it was raging over so many others lives as well.

Once I began to understand the schemes of this enemy, the more I started to see the battle I was in. The ministry the Lord was preparing me for at the time—as a high school teacher at a private Christian school—lasted for seventeen years. God's assignment to me on the first day of school was this: "I have called you to be a watchman over these students' lives. Love them and tell them the truth." He took me to Ezekiel 33:1–6 to understand what the assignment of the watchman was. I took that call to those students very seriously. I began to teach my students about the armor of God and the struggle and war we will be in all of our lives.

At the beginning of every Bible class and after prayer requests, I had them stand up and put on the pieces of the armor, with hand motions and Scriptures that went with each piece. Through all of their complaining about having to stand and put on the armor every day (☺), I knew they needed to understand another level in their walk with Jesus Christ.

Well, lo and behold, to this day, those very students have related to me how they remember the tools and the Scriptures of putting on the whole armor of God. Parents out there, even though they're complaining, your kids hear you loud and clear! Not only have they reiterated to me that they continued to put on the armor daily, but they have taught their children to do the same. I get letters from former students who are parents now, who tell me that they stand with their kids at the front door of the house, each putting on the armor of God before they leave for school. No matter the age, they all know it well. As I am writing this, out of the clear blue, one of my former students sent me a video of her kindergarten class. She has taught them the armor of God! They have memorized all the pieces, along with the Scriptures to go with them. They have way more hand motions than what I taught, but they got it! She and I laughed because she said, "I don't know if they know their ABCs, but they know the armor of God!"

Obviously, the armor of God is not just for kids. I have felt the Lord's nudging in the last year to put these tools and what I have learned about spiritual warfare and the armor of God into this book. I pray that it will help you bring the fight to where it belongs—not to a person, but to the enemy of your faith, your soul, and your life.

This is not a formula for all of our prayers to be answered or for everything to go our way. We all know that's not how God works. He takes each of our situations and circumstances and works them out for our good and His glory. The armor is a way to be clothed in Christ on a daily basis and let Him fight our battle, to give Him control. I have said so often, "Lord, I can't do this; I need Your help. I surrender. I give You control." A peace comes when we release and surrender to Him. That's the relationship He wants with us.

THE ARMOR OF GOD IS NOT A FORMULA FOR ALL OF OUR PRAYERS TO BE ANSWERED OR FOR EVERYTHING TO GO OUR WAY. THAT'S NOT HOW GOD WORKS.

It is quite imperative in the days we are living in that our quiet time, our devotional time, with the Lord is a daily activity. Prayer and worship are tools for warfare as well as the Word of God. The culture we are living in demands that we stick close to Jesus. If not, we will see ourselves battle weary with no energy to stand and fight. Worship is one of my go-to's in this warfare we are in. Worship will help win the battle and worship will help win the war. When worship goes hand in hand with prayer, the armor of God, and the Word of God, anxiety, fear, discouragement, and every other evil thing will have to flee. He promises:

> *Do not be anxious about anything, but in everything by prayer and supplication with thanksgiving let your requests be made known to God. And the peace of God, which surpasses all understanding, will guard your hearts and your minds in Christ Jesus.*
>
> (Philippians 4:6–7 ESV)

This book will challenge you to up your game in the fight. It takes courage to stay in a battle and stand, to submit to God and watch the devil flee. I have come to realize that I need to take heart in my circumstances and situations for the battle belongs to the Lord.

Bestselling author Donna VanLiere said something quite powerful during a recent interview on Cornerstone Television Network's *Hope Today* show:

> "We are falling asleep listening to the Word. The Holy Spirit is grabbing a hold of us again and again saying, 'Wake up! Wake up church! Understand that you are living in a time of signs. Look up, see what's happening. Get your face out of Facebook. Get yourself off

of Twitter. Stop watching Netflix and YouTube and Amazon Prime. Get into My Word and understand what is happening. And church, you have got to start praying.'"[1]

What a timely and prophetic word! As the church of Christ, we need to take our strong stand and get back in the fight.

A casual response to our faith will cause many casualties on the battlefield. We need to wake up in this hour we are living in and not be casual Christians. I was in prayer months ago and heard in my heart as plain as day: *Those who are not paying attention to the battle will be deceived in the fight.* And then just today, I heard very clearly: *Sins hidden in the darkness are tripping up the church.* With those two challenges, I believe God has our attention. I know He has mine. Armor up! It's time we take our stand against the enemy of our soul and finish this race, fighting this good fight of faith!

A CASUAL RESPONSE TO OUR FAITH WILL CAUSE MANY CASUALTIES ON THE BATTLEFIELD.

Stand and keep standing…and expose the darkness with His light!

---

1. "Afghanistan, End Times & Jesus' Second Coming," *Hope Today*, August 18, 2021 (www.youtube.com/watch?v=YNTZNwjHkl8).

But all things become visible when they are exposed by the light, for everything that becomes visible is light. For this reason it says, "Awake, sleeper, and arise from the dead, and Christ will shine on you."   (Ephesians 5:13–14)

ONE

WRESTLING AGAINST A SPIRITUAL FORCE

WHAT IS SPIRITUAL WARFARE?

Spiritual warfare is the wrestling with the enemy, Satan, who fights against our soul and spirit to keep us from being and doing all that we have been called to do in this life through Christ. It is resisting temptations to sin and fighting the good fight of faith to reject lies. It is referred to throughout the Old and New Testaments. Writing about spiritual warfare in his book *Angels: God's Secret Agents*, Billy Graham said, "All this comes about because the powers of darkness press their counterattack to recapture the ground held for the glory of God."[2] Read that sentence again.

As Christians, we need a clear understanding of spiritual warfare and the battle going on around us in the unseen

2. Billy Graham, *Angels: God's Secret Agents* (Nashville, TN: Thomas Nelson, Inc., 1995).

world. As a result, we will be able to grasp the spiritual clothing we will be putting on with the armor of God.

Satan hates God and wants to disrupt everything good that God has placed upon this life and upon His children. Jesus did warn us, *"Be of sober spirit, be on the alert. Your adversary, the devil, prowls around **like** a roaring lion, seeking someone to devour"* (1 Peter 5:8). We are to be aware and vigilant of this enemy who prowls and roars *like* a lion. Jesus is the Lion of the Tribe of Judah. Satan is the great counterfeit, prowling about *like* a roaring lion. Satan is absolutely nothing like the King of Kings and Lord of Lords, although he tries to make people think otherwise. Always keep in mind, *"even Satan disguises himself as an angel of light"* (2 Corinthians 11:14). You can't fight a spiritual war with emotions or the flesh for you will become a casualty very quickly. Satan has no new tricks. He is not to be feared; he is to be dealt with by the power of the Word of God.

YOU CAN'T FIGHT A SPIRITUAL WAR WITH EMOTIONS OR THE FLESH FOR YOU WILL BECOME A CASUALTY VERY QUICKLY.

This is a crazy thought, but imagine if a snake was in your house. Yes, I know—yikes! I don't even like worms, let alone snakes. But let's just pretend there is a big snake in your house. When you kill a snake by cutting off its head, it thrashes around for a while before it finally dies. That is exactly what Satan is doing; he is a snake with its head cut off and he's thrashing around. He has been defeated by the sacrifice and resurrection of Jesus. In fact, Jesus made a public spectacle of him:

> *Having disarmed the powers and authorities, [Jesus] made a public spectacle of them, triumphing over them by the cross.*   (Colossians 2:15 NIV)

Our enemy has been defeated and he's flailing about, trying to strike at everyone and everything. But Satan has no authority unless we give it to him by agreeing with his thoughts, lies and deceptions. Don't forget who he is. *"The thief comes **only** to steal and kill and destroy; I came so that they would have life, and have it abundantly"* (John 10:10). The devil is a thief and a deceiver; his only job is to steal, kill, and destroy. Oh, and may I remind you...he doesn't fight fair.

DANIEL'S PRAYER

The main characters of the Old and New Testaments, along with those on the outskirts of the stories in the Bible, have had to fight spiritual battles over their lives. I am immediately reminded of chapter 10 in the book of Daniel.

The entire chapter is intriguing, but I am only going to touch on the warfare involved. In the first few versus, Daniel had been fasting, praying, and mourning for three entire weeks. After those three weeks, he sees a vision of a certain man dressed in linen. He goes into detail of what this man looks like. Then Scripture tells us that Daniel lost his strength and went pale at the vision of this man dressed in linen. This angelic being tells Daniel:

> *Do not be afraid, Daniel, for from the first day that you set your heart on understanding this and on humbling yourself before your God, your words were heard, and I have come in response to your words.* **But** *the prince of the kingdom of Persia was standing in my way for twenty-one days; then behold, Michael, one of the chief princes, came to help me, for I had been left there with the kings of Persia.*
>
> (Daniel 10:12–13)

Every time we see or hear the word "but" in Scripture, we need to pay attention to what comes next. Right there, it tells us that God sent His answer the moment Daniel prayed, yet his prayer was withheld in this spiritual fight for twenty-one days.

This encounter Daniel had with his prayers being held up is something you and I can relate to and learn how to fight through. If you are feeling a delay in answered prayer, it can be God's timing, something God is building in your character, or the enemy delaying it. When you are in a delay, ask the Lord where it is coming from and pray in the direction He shows you. If it's His delay, it's because He sees the big picture and is getting all players in order over your life and building character in you as well. If He shows you it's the enemy delaying, then battle through it in prayer, letting the enemy know he has no authority to thwart the plans of God for your life.

You see, when you *realize you are in a war* with an enemy that wants to deceive you, lie to you, and steal all God has in store for you, you will have the tenacity to come against that spiritual enemy. You just need the tools to do so. In the natural, we would never walk out of our homes without putting our clothes on. In just the same way, you should not walk out of the house or let your kids do so without wearing your spiritual clothes: the armor of God. And I guarantee you, when you get this and see the authority you have over the enemy of your life, it will change the way you live your Christian walk.

We will use the Word of God for every piece of the armor for that is our line of victory for every battle. You will see how important it is to understand this warfare and know these six pieces of the armor to be put on daily.

A THIEF AND A LIAR

I do not want to glorify Satan, but to expose him for who he really is: a liar and the father of lies. There is never any truth in him. *"He was a murderer from the beginning, and does not stand in the truth because there is no truth in him. Whenever he tells a lie, he speaks from his own nature, because he is a liar and the father of lies"* (John 8:44). It's Satan's nature to lie. Think about that. It's all through him to lie…he speaks lies. He is a deceiver and will do anything to throw you off the course that Jesus has for your life. It's time for him to be exposed and you know who you are fighting.

You are not in this battle alone. Jesus had to deal with the enemy; you and I will have to deal with him. Don't let yourself be isolated in the fight. Run to the Lord. We are a big family. Bring your friends, family, and church family to pray and battle through with you.

IT'S SATAN'S NATURE TO LIE. HE IS A DECEIVER AND WILL DO ANYTHING TO THROW YOU OFF THE COURSE THAT JESUS HAS FOR YOUR LIFE.

We all know that prayer is key over our lives. It moves God's hand. It brings us close to Him, to His very presence. It is powerful. It builds our relationship with Him. It brings life to our situations and answers to our heart's cry. It is our lifeline. Casual prayer is a mistake. Lethargic Christian living is something the enemy relishes because he knows we are weak when we are prayerless, and it's his favorite scheme to use against us as believers. English preacher Guy H. King (1885–1956) said, "No one is a firmer believer in the power of prayer than the devil; not that he practices it, but he suffers from it." Let that sink in!

THE STRENGTH OF HIS MIGHT

> *Finally, be strong in the Lord and in the **strength of His might**. Put on the full armor of God, so that you will be able to stand firm against the schemes of the devil.*
> (Ephesians 6:10–11)

When you look at this Scripture, you see that this battle is in the strength of *God's might*.

This is not our fight; it is the Lord's. He just wants us to stand in the battle with Him and take our authority against the powers of darkness. Jesus states, *"I have given you authority to trample on snakes and scorpions and to overcome all the power of the enemy; nothing will harm you"* (Luke 10:19 NIV). He has given us the authority to trample on the enemy. But when we come in agreement with the negative, discouraging, or fearful voices in our lives, we invite the enemy to have a hay day in our minds and emotions.

I am writing this at the time of a virus pandemic that has hit America and the world. There is much unrest in the streets of America today as well. The spirits of fear, greed, division, offense, violence, hate, and sickness have been running rampant across the country and across the world. The fear of death, disease, financial loss, the unknown, the future, and so much more has gripped the entire nation. If we do not take up our authority against these spirits that are causing such havoc, and believe that God has each of us in the very palm of His hand, we will succumb to the enemy's schemes and live in absolute torment. We need to remind ourselves that we walk in the authority and the strength of His might—His victory!

Dr. Tony Evans says, "Satan often tries to prevent you from taking the spiritual realm seriously. If he can divert your attention away from the spiritual realm, he can keep you away from the only place where your victory is found. If he can distract you with people or things you can see, taste, touch, hear, or smell, he can keep you from living a life of victory."[3]

The apostle Paul would never have told us to put this armor on if he wasn't adamant that we have an enemy who is scheming to make us weak in our faith and take us out of the plan of God and the victory He has for our lives. And don't be mistaken; the devil would love to mess not only with your gifts and calling, but with your loved ones as well. We do not want to be ignorant and not realize where the fiery darts against us are coming from. When a warrior goes into spiritual battle, he must know who his enemy is and how to defeat him. Believe it or not, it is not always from other people or your own thoughts.

WE STRUGGLE NOT AGAINST FLESH AND BLOOD

> *For our struggle is not against flesh and blood, but against the rulers, against the powers, against the world forces of this darkness, against the spiritual forces of wickedness in the heavenly places.*   (Ephesians 6:12)

I repeat, we are not wrestling against flesh and blood. Your family, your husband, your wife, your kids, your brothers or sisters, your coworkers, your friends, and your church family are not your enemy. We are wrestling against a spiritual force that wants nothing more than to pull our relationships apart and cause disunity and dissension among us. If he can, Satan

---

3. Tony Evans, *Winning Your Spiritual Battles* (Eugene, OR: Harvest House Publishers, 2011).

will use those in our lives to cause heartache. And he will infiltrate our fleshly thoughts, if we let him, to take ownership of our lives. Our flesh rises up as well and can cause a lot of confusion and chaos. We need to understand and grasp the difference between the soul and the spirit and know how to respond to them.

WHO YOU ARE DOESN'T MATTER TO SATAN; HE WILL SOW THE BAIT.

There is one fiery dart that is raging in the nation, causing us to wrestle against each other, and it most certainly includes brothers and sisters in Christ. It's the spirit of offense. This one spirit alone is tearing us apart with, "I'm offended," "No, I'm offended. You offended me," "No, you offended me," and on and on. Friends, family members, or coworkers, rich or poor, Democrat or Republican, black, white, Asian, or Hispanic—it doesn't matter to Satan; he will sow the bait. The word bait means, "to try to make angry with criticism or insults; unjust, malicious, or persistent attacks." It is causing friends and family members to no longer speak to each other. Being offended and staying offended is like drinking poison and hoping it teaches someone else a lesson. That is exactly what is going on. Author John Bevere wrote an excellent book entitled *The Bait of Satan*.[4] That bait is the spirit of offense. Here's what God says about it:

---

4. John Bevere, *The Bait of Satan* (Lake Mary, FL: Charisma House, 1994).

A brother who is offended is harder to be won than a strong city, and quarrels are like the bars of a citadel.

(Proverbs 18:19)

Don't get caught in the poison—it is a trap! See that offense for what it really is: a bait from the enemy of your very soul.

Isn't it crazy how so often the enemy is portrayed like the character we see in cartoons, a red devil with two horns? That is not the truth. I have heard people laugh and say, "I don't care if I go to hell one day; it will just be one big party." Boy, are they mistaken! That is a lie from the very pit of hell. Satan is not your buddy or your friend. He is a master deceiver, and he is very, very good at it.

We are going to pull back the veil and let the enemy know that we see what he is trying to do in our lives. We are becoming wise to his schemes and we have our eyes wide open.

STAND FIRM AGAINST THE SCHEMES OF THE DEVIL

1. **Stand Firm.** When you have done everything you know to do in prayer, in coming to God through His Word, and in releasing it all to Him, keep standing. Many times, the Lord has us wait longer than we would ever want to. Our job is to trust and believe that He is working behind the scenes on our behalf. The Lord is the one who fights our battles. He knows exactly where you are. He vindicates, so let Him. Your job is to stand—stand firm in the

strength of His might. *"You need not fight in this battle; take your position, stand and watch the salvation of the* LORD *in your behalf....' Do not fear or be dismayed; tomorrow, go out to face them, for the* LORD *is with you"* (2 Chronicles 20:17). Keep standing firm.

2. **Schemes of the Devil.** I never noticed the word *scheme* before and the impact it has over us until I heard a message on it. That message made me think about a few things regarding the devil's schemes. Scheming is devising a crafty or secret plan specifically against you, hiding so as not to be seen. Our habits, our mistakes, our sins...he is scheming. Those thoughts in your head that say you are not enough...he is scheming. Those outbursts of anger against your family...he is scheming. The discouragement over your finances that wants to transition into depression...he is scheming. This list could go on and on. He is scheming to trip us up so as to cause havoc and destroy our faith in God. He is ultimately after your faith. That should make you very angry. He is scheming. You are wrestling against powers and principalities of this dark world.

3. **"'Not by might nor by power, but by My Spirit,' says the** LORD**"** (**Zechariah 4:6**)**.** The battle will not be won by our might or our power, but completely by His Spirit. Remember, He has given us authority in His name and by His Spirit. God is faithful. He wins battles. We need to stand and watch Him

battle on our behalf. We stand and trust Him. We may get bruised and wounded here and there. There are not too many wars when soldiers come out unscathed. But you will have victory. And you will be standing.

Jesus will always counter the enemy's schemes, assuring us, "I came *to give you life* and that abundantly!" (See John 10:10.) God is our rescuer and He is for us. He wants you to experience that He is the great *"I AM"* (Exodus 3:14) and that you can depend on Him and trust Him. He is the lover of your soul, your greatest advocate and warrior. *"The LORD will fight for you, while you keep silent"* (Exodus 14:14). He has not lost a battle yet!

JESUS WILL ALWAYS COUNTER THE ENEMY'S SCHEMES. HE IS THE LOVER OF YOUR SOUL, YOUR GREATEST ADVOCATE AND WARRIOR.

A very famous story appears in the first book of Samuel starting in chapter 19, regarding King Saul, who was trying to kill David because he was jealous of him and saw that the Lord was with him. David ran from Saul for ten years! That is a very long time to be pursued by someone wanting to take your life. David never laid a hand on Saul when he had the opportunity to do so. Why did he not defend himself against King Saul's assaults upon him? The answer is very evident because of David's relationship to God. As the future king explains to his nephew Abishai, *"Do not kill him, for who can reach out with his hand against the* LORD's *anointed and remain innocent?"* (1 Samuel 26:9).

David understood this battle he was in, but he was letting God fight it for him. He was not going to be responsible for what God wanted to do in his fight with King Saul. For vengeance is the Lord's. Just as David knew, so many times in Scripture, the Lord tells us that the battle belongs to Him. Our response should be to let go of control, surrender, and let Him have it, no matter what it looks like. *"Do not fear or be dismayed because of this great multitude, for the battle is not yours but God's"* (2 Chronicles 20:15). Obviously, there will be times you and I will need to fight through our battles alongside of the Lord, and there will be times you take your stand and let God fight the battle.

A FINAL THOUGHT

Finally, in understanding this spiritual warfare that is around us, the Lord equips us with the wisdom of His Word. It is our responsibility to use the powerful tools God has given us through praise and worship, prayer, and the Word. We will see great victory in our lives by worshipping God and praying Bible verses over ourselves, our family, and our friends. Then, as we resist the devil, he will flee. Don't lose heart when it feels like things are not moving fast enough. God's got you. He has your situation in complete focus. *"Let's not become discouraged in doing good, for in due time we will reap, if we do not become weary"* (Galatians 6:9). Take God at

His Word. Come to the Him first; don't try to fight in the flesh. It is a spiritual battle…fight on God's terms, on His ground, and watch Him move!

TAKE ACTION

We are in a battle. We have to be vigilant. We must rely on our commander in chief, the captain of the host of heaven, Jesus the Christ. You do not fight your circumstances or situations in the flesh or emotions. They are fought with the Word, worship, and prayer! You are in this race to win!

WARFARE PRAYER

Lord, I come to You in the power of the Holy Spirit knowing I do not wrestle against flesh and blood, but against powers and authorities of this dark world. Help me take this battle to where it belongs and stand in the power of your strength to combat every scheme of the enemy over my life. You are the only true God. I take my stand, as You commanded me to, knowing that Satan truly has no authority over me unless I give it to him. He has been defeated by Your victory on the cross. This warfare I am fighting is a battle that rages because the powers of darkness want to recapture the ground held for the glory of God. I no longer hide in a corner over the enemy's assaults, but I take up the full armor of God. I stand robed in Your armor daily, speaking Your Word and Your promises over my life, fearless because I call on Your name that breaks every yoke and wins every battle. I worship You for the battle has always belonged to You. I choose to stand and keep standing and expose the darkness with Your glorious light. In Jesus's name, amen.

Let's get started with the armor of God and find our clothing of power! Each piece represents a part of God's strength that extends to us.

TWO

TRUTH THAT BRINGS LIFE

*Stand firm then, with the belt of truth
buckled around your waist.*
—Ephesians 6:14 NIV

GIRD YOUR LOINS WITH THE GOSPEL OF TRUTH

The truth is the first piece of the armor of God listed in Ephesians 6. We are urged to take the truth and gird our loins with it, as some Bible translations put it.

Paul is describing the type of armor that the Roman soldier would put on daily, giving us an understanding of this armor compared to the spiritual armor that we put on daily as believers prepared for battle. The soldier's belt held his sword and bands of protection for his loins. He could also tuck his tunic into his belt to shorten it before a battle.

When we are told to gird our loins, it's a call to be prepared. Paul related the belt to that of *truth*. I find it pretty amazing that the belt is around our core and it holds all the other pieces together. Truth is the core of our being, the foundation to all the other pieces of spiritual armor. Isn't that amazing? We are kept free from the enemy's lies by abiding in God's truth.

 **TRUTH IS THE CORE OF OUR BEING, THE FOUNDATION TO ALL THE OTHER PIECES OF SPIRITUAL ARMOR.**

What is truth? Scripture tells us plainly, for Jesus said, *"I am the way, and the truth, and the life"* (John 14:6) and referred to the Holy Spirit as *"the Spirit of truth"* (verse 17). Later, He told Pilate, *"For this purpose I have been born, and for this I have come into the world: to testify to the truth. Everyone who is of the truth listens to My voice"* (John 18:37).

THE VOICE OF TRUTH

Not one of us wants to be lied to. When we realize that someone has deceived us, it changes the way that relationship goes. Without the truth, there is not much we can trust. That speaks volumes to the power of truth that is Jesus. There is so much deception and twisting of the truth in our world that we need the discernment of the voice of truth to ring over the voices of lies from the enemy.

One thing you can count on: God's Word never changes on you. *"The word of our God endures forever"* (Isaiah 40:8 NIV). That is how you can refute the voice that says you are not enough, or you don't deserve to be loved. When you hear a voice that falsely accuses you, that says you are or were the problem, or you just don't have what it takes, that is not God talking to you. We must understand that God does not speak negative or condemning words over us. When you hear those words coming at you, they are not from God. They are from the liar himself.

Who told you that you are too old? Who told you that you would never love again? Who told you that your kids will never amount to anything? *Who. Told. You?* That is not God's voice. Those are Satan's lies. Train your heart with that truth. Hurtful accusations are not the truth. If we let them stay in our thoughts and emotions about ourselves, those accusations and lies can keep us bound in our situations for years, sometimes for decades—far longer than they ever need to be. There is a different voice that tells us a different story. You counter those lies with the Word of truth. Here is God's voice:

> *God is not human, that he should lie, not a human being, that he should change his mind. Does he speak and then not act? Does he promise and not fulfill?*
>
> (Numbers 23:19 NIV)

Sanctify them in the truth; Your word is truth.

(John 17:17)

The song "Voice of Truth" by the Christian rock band Casting Crowns includes these lyrics:

Out of all the voices calling out to me

I will choose to listen and believe the voice of truth[5]

The entire song is quite powerful. We have a choice to listen and believe God's voice over the world's voice, the flesh, or the enemy. It is a choice to believe the truth. God has never lied to you. We may have wrongly perceived how we wanted Him to do something or respond to a certain situation, but He has not purposefully lied to you. He has given you His Word. He wants you to believe Him and leave the results to Him.

GOD WANTS YOU TO BELIEVE HIM AND LEAVE THE RESULTS TO HIM.

For most of us, when we were kids and our parents promised us something, we didn't question it. We simply believed them. Why? Because we knew them, we trusted them, and we knew they loved us. So we didn't give it a second thought when they promised something. Why is it different with believing God? He knows everything about us.

---

5. Casting Crowns, "Voice of Truth," on *Casting Crowns* (Beach Street, 2004).

Lord, You have searched me and known me. You know when I sit down and when I get up; You understand my thought from far away. You scrutinize my path and my lying down, and are acquainted with all my ways.

(Psalm 139:1–3)

God knows you completely! You were in His sight before you were in your mother's womb. Yet so often we question His promises for us. I believe most of the time our doubts come when we don't truly know His character or His true love and heart for us. When a situation hasn't happened the way we wanted, we think that He has lied to us, or that He can't be trusted. That is simply not true! God has plans far above what we do for our own lives. It is time to believe His voice of truth over the enemy's voice of lies and deception.

Start changing how you respond to those voices. Speak the truth of His Word. I have index cards with Scripture verses written on them that I keep with me at all times to remind me to speak God's Word over my life. I keep pouring truth over myself because the lies against the truth come in all directions—for all of us. Satan attacks truth with lies. He especially focuses on attacking God's promises by casting doubt on God's goodness toward you.

 SATAN ATTACKS TRUTH WITH LIES, ESPECIALLY ATTACKING GOD'S PROMISES BY CASTING DOUBT ON GOD'S GOODNESS TOWARD YOU.

GOD VS. THE GREAT DECEIVER

Remember in the garden of Eden, when God told Adam, *"You are free to eat from any tree in the garden; but you must not eat from the tree of the knowledge of good and evil, for when you eat from it you will certainly die"* (Genesis 2:16–17 NIV). There was a reason why God did not want Adam and Eve to eat from that one tree. They could eat freely from every other tree. God wasn't keeping anything good from them. He was allowing them to have access to all the blessings. Yet the deceiver came in so sneaky with that one temptation. Satan used God's words to trip up Adam and Eve when he came knocking on their lives to deceive, destroy, and bring about the fall of man.

I know we have heard this story a million times, but let's look with a new perspective. Let's pull it apart.

Satan starts a conversation with Eve: *"Has God really said, 'You shall not eat from any tree of the garden'?"* (Genesis 3:1). The question and Eve's response changed the entire course of human history. By causing Eve to doubt God's Word, Satan brought evil into the world.

> *The woman said to the serpent, "From the fruit of the trees of the garden we may eat; but from the fruit of the tree which is in the middle of the garden, God has said, 'You shall not eat from it **or touch it**, or you will die.'"*
>
> (Genesis 3:2–3)

Look how Eve added to God's Word, suggesting He said they could not even touch the tree's fruit, distorting His

TRUTH THAT BRINGS LIFE   47

direction and showing that the serpent's subtle challenge was working its poison. Satan made Eve question God and doubt what He said. How often we are prone to give the same response at the craftiness of the enemy over our own lives.

Let's read on because Satan is not done; he is going in for the kill by using God's own words.

The serpent said to the woman, "You certainly will not die! For God knows that on the day you eat from it your eyes will be opened, and you will become like God, knowing good and evil."   (Genesis 3:4–5)

Satan telling Eve that she *"certainly will not die"* was a blatant denial of God's divine truth. When he suggested that *"God knows,"* Satan accused God of having untrustworthy motives. The great deceiver insinuated a falsehood. We must be vigilant of his craftiness in all areas of our lives. He completely turned the conversation God had with them, twisting it and turning it around to fit his narrative. Sound familiar?

After they responded to the enemy's lies, Adam and Eve's eyes were opened. Look at the three things that came into their lives immediately: shame, fear, and hiding. Shame from their nakedness; fear of what God would say; and hiding from His response to their disobedience. My, my, how this has never stopped since the day Adam and Eve fell to sin in the garden! Satan is as crafty, subtle, and conniving to us as he was to them. He still uses shame, fear, and hiding in a very effective way. This is not a game. This is spiritual warfare that Satan has no intention of fighting fair. It is imperative that we know the Word of truth and wrap it firmly around our waist like a belt to gird ourselves with what God says about circumstances in our lives and not the enemy's narrative.

IT IS IMPERATIVE THAT WE KNOW THE WORD OF TRUTH AND WRAP IT FIRMLY AROUND OUR WAIST LIKE A BELT.

I am reminded of the lies and false accusations Jesus had to endure in His trial before His crucifixion. The entire trial was a sham. They had nothing to build their case on except to falsely accuse Him. Look at what Jesus was dealing with: He was mocked; betrayed by a friend; sold for thirty pieces of silver; forsaken by His disciples; accused by false witnesses while He stood silently in front of His accusers; and beaten, spat upon, and rejected. He knows what it is like to be lied about, mistrusted, betrayed, rejected, and doubted. The very Son of God, who came to heal a broken world, was accused of something He never did. How much more proof do we need to know that we *must* and *can* run to Him and find love and strength in His powerful arms when we go through so many of the same things? He understands.

SIN THAT SEPARATES

This *belt of truth* also involves unconfessed sin that separates you and me from fellowship with God. In this hour, the heavens are crying for us to come clean and repent before the Lord. It's time to stop living a casual Christian life.

> *Repent, then, and turn to God, so that your sins may be wiped out, that times of refreshing may come from the Lord.*
>
> (Acts 3:19 NIV)

God forgives you the moment you ask for forgiveness. The slate is wiped clean. Sin and shame are the devil's poison. He knows how it captures our very souls.

Jesus has not given us shame. He has delivered us from all that has tried to suffocate us with chains of sin that hinder. *"You have been set free from sin and have become slaves to righteousness"* (Romans 6:18 NIV).

We are to confess and turn from the sin that easily entangles us and weakens us in our faith. Think about that…the sins that entangle us are weakening our faith, making us null and void to the purposes of our lives and stopping us from living out the freedom Jesus gave us.

> *Let's rid ourselves of every obstacle and the sin which so easily entangles us, and let's run with endurance the race that is set before us, looking only at Jesus, the originator and perfecter of the faith, who for the joy set before Him endured the cross, despising the shame, and has sat down at the right hand of the throne of God.*
>
> (Hebrews 12:1–2)

Repent! God has need of you in this hour. He needs you to get untangled and stay untangled from the familiar sins that have you bound. Replace the entanglement with the truth of His Word. In his famous sermon "Sinners in the Hands of an Angry God," theologian Jonathan Edwards said of the unrepented, "Their foot shall slide in due time." God is calling us in these days of trouble and darkness to repent from the sins and habits that are holding us bound. Stop your foot from slipping for today is the day of salvation!

A FINAL THOUGHT

Fix your eyes on Jesus! Fix your eyes on Jesus! Stay steadfast in your pursuit of Him. Let His presence and His truths heal your soul. Let His love absorb your heart. Let Him reveal Himself to you in a unique and powerful way. Take seriously the lies and deception that are running rampant around you and ask the Lord for His discernment to expose them and bring you truth. Let His voice of truth ring out through your life and cause every lie to shrivel up around you. By abiding in the truth, walking in the truth, and speaking the truth, you will have grasped the core of your spiritual walk.

> *It was not by their sword that they won the land, nor did their arm bring them victory; it was your right hand, your arm, and the light of your face, for you loved them.*
>
> (Psalm 44:3 NIV)

Let's put into action what you have learned. Armor up before you leave the house in the morning.

TAKE ACTION

This action you are about to participate in will be for all the pieces of the armor, yet with different Scriptures. Remember, this *belt of truth* holds all the other pieces of the armor in place!

When you stand up, putting on the armor for this first piece, *say out loud* while you are using the motion of putting a belt around your waist, "I gird my loins with the gospel of truth. Jesus is the way, and the truth, and the life; no one comes to the Father but by Him."

WARFARE PRAYER

Lord, You are the voice of truth. The truth of Your Word is the core of my being. I wrap Your truth around me and stand against the taunting lies of the enemy. I take full authority and come out of agreement with every lie that tries to speak to my heart, spirit, and mind. I come in agreement and open my ears to hear what the Spirit of the Lord is saying to me about myself, my family, and my friends by the power of the Holy Spirit. Your Word is truth. When I recognize the lies fighting to get back into my heart and spirit, help me to take them captive according to Your Word and shut the mouth of lions. I know how much I am loved by You. Fill me, Lord, today with the power of Your Holy Spirit afresh and anew to speak life and truth over every fiber of my inner man. In Jesus's name, amen.

THREE

RIGHT STANDING BEFORE GOD

And having put on the breastplate of righteousness.
—Ephesians 6:14

PUT ON THE BREASTPLATE OF RIGHTEOUSNESS

The breastplate protects vital organs like the heart and lungs. Without it, any attack could be fatal; with it, an attack to the torso could be rendered ineffective. *"The breastplate of righteousness"* that Paul mentions in this Scripture protects the heart.

In understanding this as a piece of the armor of God, the breastplate of righteousness means you are called and chosen to live a free life in Christ. You are in right standing with

Him. That's why the enemy takes shots at your heart. When God looks at you, He sees you blameless before Him because you carry the righteousness His Son purchased for you on the cross, nailing your sins there. Our own righteousness is not sufficient to protect us.

This breastplate protects our spiritual heart, soul, desires, and emotions from the deception of the evil one. We need to do some real soul searching to see what we are feeding our hearts on a daily basis.

GUARD YOUR HEART

Proverbs 4:23 (NIV) says very specifically, *"Above all else, guard your heart, for everything you do flows from it."* To guard is to protect; we are to protect our heart from the onslaught coming our way on a daily basis, and to do it diligently, with energetic effort. This is a work that we all need to do. To guard and protect our heart, with this breastplate of righteousness, is necessary to live this walk we have in Christ. For from our heart flows all of the issues of life.

I ask this question: Are we allowing things into our lives and our hearts that are contrary to God's Word? The enemy of God schemes to keep us entrapped in our own mess, or in the mess he has devised against us. The sinful habits that hold us captive and those things that the enemy entices us with are meant to dull our hearts to the truth of who we are in Christ. Satan accuses us constantly. We all have made mistakes in our lives. We all have felt the guilt of something we wish we could take back. God is not holding anything against any of us. That is not who He is. Christ's death on the cross washed away our sins and made us right with Him. The accuser wants to keep us bound even after God has forgiven us. We must put on this breastplate of righteousness to receive and believe we are forgiven and nullify the accuser. *"For the accuser of our brothers and sisters has been thrown down, the one who accuses them before our God day and night"* (Revelations 12:10).

YOU ARE NOT YOUR SIN

When we have sinned and repented before God and asked for forgiveness, we are made clean before Him. *You are not your sin.* Let me say that again, you are not your sin. When I understood this and had an *aha* moment, my whole life changed. I understood that God saw me, His beloved child, and not my sin. The answer was right in the Word.

> *He* [God] *made Him who knew no sin* [Jesus] *to be sin in our behalf, so that we might become the righteousness of God in Him.*   (2 Corinthians 5:21)

You know how when you read the Scriptures so often, you can easily bypass the richest parts? Well, I had read this verse for years and never saw the revelation. Then one day the revelation hit me so hard, it changed me forever. Jesus became that sin you are carrying and nailed it to the cross. It is not yours. When you confess, repent, and ask for forgiveness, it is no longer yours. He became sin for us. You are not your sin… Jesus became it and took it. That's His righteousness for us.

So when God looks at you, He doesn't see that sin; He sees the blood of Jesus over it.

The enemy of our soul accuses and deceives us into thinking we are not clean or whole, but just because you don't feel clean doesn't mean you're not! When we have sat in our sin for a long time and are finally free, we may not *feel* free right away. That's why we don't live by our feelings but by faith. The Word must be on our tongue so that we can continue to remind the enemy that we were forgiven the moment we asked. *"As far as the east is from the west, so far has He removed our wrongdoings from us"* (Psalm 103:12).

YOU ARE NOT YOUR SIN. JUST BECAUSE YOU DON'T FEEL CLEAN DOESN'T MEAN YOU'RE NOT!

I heard the following story a long time ago and it has stuck with me ever since. I think you will get the analogy and I pray it sticks with you as well:

THE TRAINED ELEPHANT

When a baby elephant is being trained in a circus, it is tethered to a stake in the ground with a very thick rope. When the baby elephant tries to get free, it is unsuccessful. After a while, the elephant realizes that the rope will always be too strong…and so it gives up.

As the elephant grows to its full size, it remembers how it wasted its energy trying to escape captivity. Now the trainer can tether the elephant with a slender thread tied to a much smaller stake, and the elephant will make no attempt to escape to freedom. Yet in reality, it could break free with one flinch of its foot. Wow.

Like the elephant, when we are sitting in our sin for so long, tethered by Satan, and then ask God for forgiveness, He frees us as soon as we ask...but we don't feel free. We stay tethered to that sin, not realizing the freedom that is ours through Christ. Satan gets us so caught in our feelings and emotions that we think we are not free. In reality, the moment you asked for forgiveness, you were free.

WE STAY TETHERED TO THAT SIN, NOT REALIZING THE FREEDOM THAT IS OURS THROUGH CHRIST.

*Come now, let us reason together, says the L*ORD*: though your sins are like scarlet, they shall be as white as snow; though they are red like crimson, they shall become like wool.* (Isaiah 1:18 ESV)

Jesus loves us and welcomes us to join Him, as noted in the lyrics to this song by Sidewalk Prophets:

He said come to the table

Come join the sinners who have been redeemed

Take your place beside the Savior

Sit down and be set free[6]

Regardless of our failures, His righteousness has been credited to our account. We make Him and His ways our dwelling place, desiring for His ways to be ours. This allows the Holy Spirit to come and live within us. The Holy Spirit now gives you and me the life and power to live above sin. He imparts in you godly living. That is the breastplate of righteousness. Have we fully grasped it?

GOD'S GRACE AND FORGIVENESS

The story that immediately comes to mind is the woman caught in adultery in John 8:1–11. Jesus was teaching in the temple area and *"all the people were coming to Him"* (verse2) when the scribes and Pharisees—the religious legal "experts"—brought a woman caught in the very act of adultery and placed her in the center of the courtyard, in front of everyone. Have you ever had a secret you never wanted anyone to know about that was somehow exposed? This woman was in that situation. So not only feeling shame, standing alone in her sin, I'm sure she was quite frightened, knowing that being caught in this act meant she would be stoned to death.

---

6. Sidewalk Prophets, "Come to the Table," on *Something Different* (Word Records, 2015).

I visualize her being wrapped in a dirty bedsheet thrown over her, trying to cover her nakedness. The scribes and Pharisees brought this woman to Jesus's attention so that they might have grounds for accusing Him. They badgered him with their persistent questions. Isn't it funny how the enemy is like that, always grinding away in an effort to trap us?

But instead of answering them, Jesus stooped down and wrote on the ground with His finger. No one knows what He was writing. We can all speculate. John, the writer of this Scripture, never said. Most scholars believe Jesus was writing the sins of the scribes and Pharisees. As they continued to ask Him about this woman, Jesus straightened up and said to them, *"He who is without sin among you, let him be the first to throw a stone at her"* (verse 7). Then He stooped down and kept writing on the ground.

What an incredible response from a merciful God! He doesn't argue with them. He doesn't have a conversation about it with them. He simply turns the tide and puts the response back on them.

One by one, these men dropped their stones and began to walk away from the woman. Because of Jesus's response to them, they had no reason to accuse or condemn her. And watch what Jesus, her righteousness, did for her. He straightened up and she, frightened and trembling, stood there with Him.

Jesus said to her, "Woman, where are they? Did no one condemn you?" She said, "No one, Lord." And Jesus said, "I do not condemn you, either. Go. From now on do not sin any longer."   (John 8:10–11)

Jesus acknowledges what she has done is sin. But He doesn't yell at her, saying, "What's the matter with you? You should have known better!" Instead of accusing and condemning her, He offers her freedom. His love and compassion for her sets her free—just as His love and compassion does for you. Instead of death, she receives His grace. Instead of condemnation, she receives His forgiveness. Instead of carrying the identity of being an adulterer, she becomes a daughter and a follower of the King.

What a beautiful story of grace through forgiveness. That's what Jesus offers us through the breastplate of righteousness, which protects our heart from sin and teaches us how to walk in His ways. When we tolerate sin, refuse to forgive, rely on personal righteousness, or allow earthly concerns to distract our time for an intimate relationship with the Lord, we, in effect, take off the breastplate of righteous, minimizing its power to protect us. When we say *no* to God in an area He wants us to work on, we open a crack in the armor where Satan's arrows can get through. That's why we need to remain diligent in guarding our heart and being obedient when the Lord wants to draw us away from the noise so that we can heal.

A FINAL THOUGHT

We must never forget that God's love and forgiveness are free. He has cleansed us from all unrighteousness by Jesus's willingness to take our dirt and sins and make them His own, nailing them to the cross so we can be free once and for all.

WE CAN BOLDLY COME BEFORE GOD TO OBTAIN MERCY AND FIND GRACE TO HELP US IN OUR TIME OF NEED.

Just because we are Christians doesn't make us immune from sin. It's in putting on His righteousness that He has the power to heal us from our sin. He not only forgives us, but He can show us the very root of sin, the nature in us that causes us to be tempted to sin. Many people try by their own willpower to resist sin in their lives, only to find, time and time again, the lack of power to resist the temptations of the enemy's arrows, and they fall back to that very sin.

When we realize that sin, whether by thought, word, or deed, is too hard to overcome, we have our answer: *"Let us therefore come boldly to the throne of grace, that we may obtain mercy and find grace to help in time of need"* (Hebrews 4:16 NKJV). We can boldly come before Him. He sends us His Holy Spirit to help and guide us in the moment of temptation. You will never leave the throne room of grace empty; His righteousness will give you power to resist sin until it is destroyed. May we never use His righteousness, grace, or forgiveness as a license to keep sinning, but rather as the key to overcoming sin!

> *For sin shall not be master over you, for you are not under the Law but under grace. What then? Are we to sin because we are not under the Law but under grace? Far from it!*
> (Romans 6:14–15)

> *It was for freedom that Christ set us free; therefore keep standing firm and do not be subject again to a yoke of slavery.*
> (Galatians 5:1)

TAKE ACTION

Remember, this breastplate of righteousness makes you blameless before God!

When you stand up, putting on the armor of God for this second piece, *say out loud* while crossing your arms over your chest, "The breastplate of righteousness. I am in right standing before God because of what Jesus has done for me."

WARFARE PRAYER

Lord, I am overwhelmed by You. You have taken my sins, all of them, and nailed them to the cross. You never throw them in my face, for You have thrown them as far as the east is from the west and You remember them no more. You made a way through so I can live healed and whole. You exchanged my unrighteousness for Your righteousness. Hope is never lost with You. You exposed and defeated the great deceiver. I love You, Lord. I thank You that You have called me to walk in freedom. You love me so much that you made sure I didn't have to live apart from You in despair over my own entangled sins. I put on this breastplate of righteousness and guard my heart from every attack of the enemy who thrives on calling me guilty and shameful. I know now that when God looks at me, He sees me blameless before Him because of the shed blood of Jesus Christ. I praise You this day and stand in Your righteousness and forgiving grace. In Jesus's name, amen.

FOUR

PEACE FOR YOUR HEART

And having strapped on your feet the preparation
of the gospel of peace.
—Ephesians 6:15

WEAR THE GOSPEL OF PEACE ON YOUR FEET

The soles of the sandals worn by Roman soldiers were studded with hobnails, which gave them firm footing on uneven, rough, or wet terrain and enabled them to hold their ground when fighting. These battle shoes in the Spirit are purposely used to give you *"the peace of God, which transcends all understanding"* (Philippians 4:7 NIV). Meaning, *"Trust in the LORD with all of your heart and* **do not lean on your own** *understanding*" (Proverbs 3:5). You dig your shoes into the ground, no matter how scary the circumstance, and trust His Word. Easier said than done, I know, but let's journey further to get some understanding.

WE LOSE OUR PEACE WHEN WE LOSE OUR TRUST IN GOD.

Having peace has so much to do with trusting and believing God. We lose our peace when we lose our trust. I just learned that lesson in my own life recently. The moment I stopped trusting God, I lost my peace. God is not haphazard with your life. He knows you. He cares. He sees you. He knows when you are in a place of anguish, fear, mistrust, discouragement, or lost hope. We must keep coming back to the place of knowing that He has destroyed the authority of chaos and is crushing it under our feet. Chaos is the enemy's specialty because it causes unrest and steals our peace. Jesus offers you Himself so that you stop and let His peace rest on you.

> *Peace I leave you, My peace I give you; not as the world gives, do I give to you. Do not let your hearts be troubled, nor fearful.*   (John 14:27)

It's not the world's rest, which is so often laced with anxiety and the belief you have to fix the situation yourself. His rest is when you are above your circumstances, knowing that the battle you are in belongs to the Lord. His peace keeps you calm in the midst of many storms.

PEACE OVER FEAR

Fear has captivated the nation. It is running rampant in every culture, in every household. It is paralyzing both Christians and non-Christians alike. But Jesus has spoken so many times in His Word: *"Fear not!"* There's a time where the spirit of fear has to face God.

> *Do not fear, for I am with you; do not be afraid, for I am your God. I will strengthen you, I will also help you, I will also uphold you with My righteous right hand.*
>
> (Isaiah 41:10)

I have spoken this verse over my life hundreds of times. It is deep in my spirit. It is a promise that I hold onto. God promises that He is with us. We are not to anxiously look about us in fear because He says, *"I am your God."* Do you see that? He is *your* God. He is with you individually and personally. He knows you by name: *"I have redeemed you; I have called you by name; you are Mine!"* (Isaiah 43:1).

When you cry out to Him with your situation, He promises to strengthen, help, and uphold you with His righteous right hand. What an amazing promise! But you must believe Him and rest those fears and cares in this promise. I know it's easier said than done; I get it. But I also know that it works when we rest in His peace over the anxiety our flesh is feeling.

There are hundreds of times God's Word tells us, *"Fear not!"* Pick which ones you want to stand on, speak them out loud daily, and stand. When you exalt the Lord over your fear, you destroy the authority of fear and peace comes. We give the spirit of fear the authority by coming into agreement with it instead of trusting God with our circumstances.

We are not very different than the disciples who walked with Jesus on the earth. Let's look at a very familiar story. In Mark 4:35–41, Jesus had just spoken to a large crowd by the sea on the parable of the sower and the soils. When He finished speaking to them and gave an explanation of the parable to His disciples, He told them to get into the boat, saying, *"Let's go over to the other side"* (verse 35). Little did they know what is about to come upon them on their way or over there! They also had no clue what lesson Jesus was going to show them about peace over fear.

While in the boat, a fierce storm came upon them. The wind was raging and the waves crashed into the boat, filling it with water. This storm frightened them to their very core. They believed beyond a shadow of a doubt that they were going to die. What kind of storm in your life have you lost your peace over? What is it that you believe or believed would ruin you? Take you out? Brought fear so strong upon your heart that it paralyzed you? That's how they were feeling. In the midst of this mighty storm, what was Jesus doing? He was *"in the stern, asleep on the cushion"* (verse 38). One disciple may have said, "He is asleep, guys! He is completely at peace." Why? Not because He was the Son of God, but because He knew who He belonged to. He knew His Father, He trusted

Him…and He was at total peace. This is the peace that passes understanding that God wants us to have in the midst of our storms.

HE CALMS THE STORMS

Once, when I was getting medical tests done and was a bit nervous about it, a good friend told me, "He is in you and He is calm." That calmed me down immediately because I redirected my focus from my anxiety about the tests to the truth that Jesus is calm in my storms. I say it to myself now whenever I feel anxious or fearful. Like those heavy sandals that the Roman soldiers wore, your shoes of peace are studded with the faithfulness of our risen Savior, who calms every storm of life.

OUR RISEN SAVIOR IS WITHIN YOU AND HE CALMS EVERY STORM OF LIFE.

Then they cried to the LORD in their trouble, and He brought them out of their distresses. He caused the storm to be still, so that the waves of the sea were hushed.
(Psalm 107:28–29)

Continuing with the story of Jesus in the boat, the disciples *"woke Him and said to Him, 'Teacher, do You not care that we are perishing?'"* (Mark 4:38). I always wondered if they needed to shake Him awake or if their loud voices of fear woke Him up. They were with the very Son of God, and yet they accused Him of not caring about them. Sadly, how many of us do the same? Even if you consider yourself a *seasoned saint*—one who has walked with the Lord a very long time— how many times have you yelled at the Lord, "Do You not care? Can't you see what this is doing to me? Why don't You care?" I know He understands when we react that way, but I so want my response to storms to be that of trust and peace, not fear and doubt!

Jesus didn't yell at them for their accusation of not caring. Scripture says, *"He got up and rebuked the wind and said to the sea, 'Hush, be still.' And the wind died down and it became perfectly calm. And He said to them, 'Why are you afraid? Do you still have no faith?'"* (verses 39–40). He asks us the same questions. Then He responds to us, saying, "Look to Me and do not be afraid."

Jesus spoke and everything went calm…everything became perfectly still! He spoke! Please understand, as you speak His Word, which is alive and active, over the storms in your life, you will experience that calm in your heart and spirit. You have the same authority as Jesus did to speak to the storms in your life because the Holy Spirit resides in you.

Truly, truly I say to you, the one who believes in Me, the works that I do, he will do also; and greater works than these he will do; because I am going to the Father.

(John 14:12)

That peace may not come immediately. Stay with it; you have the authority in His name to calm the storms in your heart when you go to His Word. It's so full of life-giving truths that you can speak out loud as often as you wish, even if it is twenty times a day or more. It is the spoken Word that will not come back void without accomplishing what it was sent out to do. I always add worship when I am in a storm. Remember, worship is warfare.

I don't make light of the storms in our lives. I know they can be difficult, even excruciating, but we do *not* need to go through them in fear. Fear is not of God. When you and I are fearful, that is our first indication that this spirit is not of God. He did not give us fear. Unfortunately, I understand this very well, for fear was something that I grew up with. I know many of you can relate to that. It has taken me years and years to put these truths into practice. I realized I had a trust issue with God. Once I got it settled in my heart that He was trustworthy, I saw how fear can dissipate.

AS TRUST AND PEACE GO HAND IN HAND, SO DO FEAR AND DOUBT.

As trust and peace go hand in hand, so do fear and doubt. Satan is no dummy; he is a bully and he loves for us to walk in fear. When he can trap us in fear, he knows we will start accusing God and our faith will start to diminish. Remember, we are in warfare. Satan does not fight fair. Don't get pushed off the battlefield because of fear. Stand strong with the gospel of peace on your feet. Fear is a spirit and it must bow to the authority of the Word of God. That's why you speak it out loud!

When Satan can rob us of our peace, he will steal our joy, our confidence, our trust, and our dependence on our good, good God. Do you see how these shoes of peace are vital component of the armor of God? It's a battle that can be won; our Lord Jesus Christ, the Prince of Peace, has already emerged triumphant!

Here are a few more Scriptures regarding peace that you can write down on index cards and speak over your life when storms in life come knocking:

> *For the mind set on the flesh is death, but the mind set on the Spirit is life and peace.* (Romans 8:6)

> *Now may the Lord of peace Himself continually grant you peace in every circumstance. The Lord be with you all!* (2 Thessalonians 3:16)

> *You will keep him in perfect peace, whose mind is stayed on You, because he trusts in You.* (Isaiah 26:3 NKJV)

A FINAL THOUGHT

No one can give you true peace. You can't muster it up. True peace comes from knowing and trusting God in a personal relationship—in knowing that *you know that you know* that He's got you and He will not leave you or forsake you. Please know that He means that. For months, I have been saying all throughout the day, "Lord, You brought me this far. You are not about to let me go now." It brings great peace to say this and know it in your heart. It puts all of the results of our prayers onto Him. We are not in control, my friends. He is. He knows what He is doing through every avenue of our lives. He is not confused about the purposes of your life or where He is leading you.

Surrender to His process, even when it feels really hard. In a recent Instagram post, Kathy Troccoli said, "Surrendering has become so much more of a friend to me. Instead of being in a tug of war with God...may surrender, this year, be a closer friend." I have made that my theme this new year. We will experience His great peace when we learn to surrender to Him—surrender our circumstances, situations, and troubled heart and spirit into the very capable hands of a mighty God. We can trust Him. *"Trust in the* LORD *forever, for in* GOD *the* LORD, *we have an everlasting Rock"* (Isaiah 26:4).

So are you ready to shod your feet, and get a secure foothold, with the shoes of peace?

Too many people do not know what it is like to walk in this peace and therefore get bombarded by heavy artillery from the enemy, causing them great anxiety and unnecessary fear. Dig those shoes in daily and rest in His arms of peace.

TAKE ACTION

When you stand up, putting on the armor of God for this third piece, *say out loud* as you swipe your hand over each of your feet, one at a time, "I shod my feet with the gospel of peace. Peace I leave you, My peace I give you; not as the world gives, do I give to you. Let not your heart be troubled nor let it be fearful."

WARFARE PRAYER

Lord, You are my Prince of Peace. You have promised me that the peace that passes understanding will guard my heart and mind as I trust in You. I know that fear is the opposite of peace. You have called fear a spirit that You have not given to me. So fear has no affect or place upon my life. I choose to walk in peace with You in every aspect of my life. I no longer give the enemy a foothold over every lofty thing that raises its ugly head against me, or robs me of my relationship with You. I stand against the enemy's ploy to trip me up and condemn me with doubts and fears. I choose, Lord, in every storm of my life, to come to You, the Prince of Peace. I cast my cares upon You, and find calm in every situation or circumstance. I tighten these shoes of peace and walk freely with my God. In Jesus's name, amen.

FIVE

STRONG IN FAITH

In addition to all, taking up the shield of faith with
which you will be able to extinguish all
the flaming arrows of the evil one.
—Ephesians 6:16

TAKE UP THE SHIELD OF FAITH

The Roman shield was a central part of the soldier's defense. It was typically made of wood that was then covered with canvas and leather. It could be doused with water to protect it against the flaming arrows of the enemy's archers.

In some translations of this verse, Paul says the shield of faith is to be taken up *"above all."* It's needed to defend against the fiery arrows of the evil one. As I shared earlier, these burning arrows come in so many forms—doubt, unbelief, rejection, evil thoughts strongly injected into the mind, or words like "you will never be healed," "you don't matter," "you're not good enough," "you have disappointed God," or "you've been forgotten"…and this can go on and on and on. The shield of faith is the armor that God has given us to defend against those burning arrows. Faith in Jesus is our shield. And all of those fiery darts can bounce off of the shield as we lift up His name and His Word against them.

WITHOUT FAITH, IT IS IMPOSSIBLE TO PLEASE GOD

Years ago, I was at a women's conference with friends. Right before I went to sit down, I heard the Lord say to my heart, "What is it about Me you don't trust?" I replied, "What?" And I heard again, "What is it about Me you don't trust?" I told my friends I needed to run to the car to get my Bible, which I had forgotten, and as I was walking up the aisle of the church, I began to cry. I whispered to the Lord, "I knew that You knew I do not trust You."

I HEARD THE LORD SAY TO MY HEART, "WHAT IS IT ABOUT ME YOU DON'T TRUST?"

That whole day, I was so quiet that my friends noticed it. I told no one what the Lord asked me, and I had no answer to His question. However, when I woke up the next morning, still crying, I had my answer. I said, "Lord, I don't believe You can or want to answer the desires of my heart." I did not trust Him and He knew it. Since that day, the Lord and I began the greatest trust and faith walk I have ever been on. It has taken years to develop, and I'm still in the process, as we all are. But it has changed me. *He* has changed me.

> *And without faith it is impossible to please God, because anyone who comes to him must believe that he exists and that he rewards those who earnestly seek him.*
> (Hebrews 11:6 NIV)

I know this piece of the armor of God, the shield of faith, is not easy to pick up in our lives. It is very hard to stand, hard to wait, and hard to trust. It is hard to not get the answer you want. It is hard to believe without seeing. It is hard to see someone not getting well. It is hard to see a loved one who has not yet committed their life to Christ. *It is hard.* That's why it is called *faith.* That is why we climb into His arms and trust His goodness. *"Now faith is the substance of things hoped for, the evidence of things not seen"* (Hebrews 11:1 KJV).

RAISING THE SHIELD OF FAITH

Have you stood on a promise of God for years? Have you stopped believing that very thing would ever come to pass? There is no formula where our faith is concerned. It's so easy to lose hope and give up when we haven't seen any movement in areas for which we have prayed for a few months or many years. When a fiery dart from the evil one hits us and we lose hope that things are not going to change, we lose faith. When we lose hope, we lose that shield of faith that we need to protect our hearts and the enemy worms his way in. Don't talk yourself out of your faith because you don't see signs of change. *God* is faithful!

Despair is a fiery dart that Satan flings at many people. Despair puts us in a place where hope is absent. The evil one wants you to live in hopelessness and despair. But almighty God, filled with all power, goodness, and love, wants us to be hopeful that things will change with His help. He answers through His Word, which is Himself.

We all know that King David had many ups and downs in his life. He speaks them out so readily in the Psalms. This one has so much truth for us on this topic of despair:

> *I would have despaired had I not believed that I would see the goodness of the LORD in the land of the living. Wait for and confidently expect the LORD; be strong and let your heart take courage; yes, wait for and confidently expect the LORD.*
>
> (Psalm 27:13–14 AMP)

David was saying, "Heart, take courage." I love that. Look up, straight at our Lord. Take courage because all things are possible with God. His goodness is all around us. He meets us everywhere we are struggling and promises an answer to our heart's despair. Wait on Him. Don't allow your hope to turn to despair; it is a lie and a fiery arrow aimed at your faith. Wait upon the Lord. He promises that you will see His goodness. He will bring you through. Lay it down at His feet and trust Him.

The lyrics of Natalie Grant's song "King of the World" immediately came to mind. Look at these lines from the chorus:

When did I forget that you've always been
The king of the world?
I try to take life back right out of the hands
Of the king of the world[7]

When did we forget that God was greater than our enemy? When did we forget that He was the King over our lives? When did we forget that He is the One who holds it all? Lift up and hold out that shield of faith!

FIGHT DISCOURAGEMENT

Let me address discouragement as it also is a great fiery dart that the enemy uses against our faith. It keeps us in a mode of unbelief and great doubt.

DISCOURAGEMENT IS A GREAT FIERY DART THAT THE ENEMY USES AGAINST OUR FAITH TO CAUSE UNBELIEF AND DOUBT.

---

7. Natalie Grant, "King of the World," on *Be One* (Curb Records, 2015).

I am sure many of you have seen the Christmas movie *It's a Wonderful Life*.[8] I love that movie. In it, an angel named Clarence tries to earn his wings by helping someone on earth. A senior angel named Joseph assigns him to help a man named George Bailey. When Clarence asks if George needs help because he is physically sick, Joseph's answer is one of the most important lines in the movie: "No, worse. He's discouraged."

Discouragement can feel like a sickness. In the dire state of discouragement, we end up losing hope, faith, and trust. The Bible speaks so readily about discouragement.

> *The LORD is the one who is going ahead of you; He will be with you. He will not desert you or abandon you. Do not fear and do not be dismayed.* (Deuteronomy 31:8)

Discouragement is a fiery dart that hits all of us, some worse than others. I used to live in discouragement. No more. The root of discouragement has been cut off. You don't have to live in discouragement for weeks, months, or years. Remember, it is a lie coming at you from Satan. It is out to steal your faith in God, to cause you to mistrust Him. It causes depression. It can be defeated when you and I put on the confident hope we have in Jesus. We can extinguish this tormenting, fiery dart when we raise up a standard against that dart with our shield of faith. "*When the enemy shall come in like a flood, the Spirit of the LORD shall lift up a standard*

---

8. *It's a Wonderful Life*, directed by Frank Capra (1946; RKO Radio Pictures).

against him" (Isaiah 59:19 KJV). Use His Word. The enemy loses when we proclaim the Word, but you must *use* it.

TACKLING THIS SHIELD OF FAITH

Jesus told His disciples, "*If you have faith the size of a mustard seed, you will say to this mountain, 'Move from here to there,' and it will move; and nothing will be impossible for you*" (Matthew 17:20). God is not asking us to have great faith or perfect faith, but He is asking us to have faith as small as a mustard seed.

A mustard seed is the smallest of seeds yet grows into the largest of trees. That means our faith grows with time and also through our experiences of life. That's why to stay in a state of discouragement defeats the very thing God may be trying to do—grow your faith. He promises in His Word:

> *He* [God] *has said,* "*I will never* [under any circumstances] *desert you* [nor give you up nor leave you without support, nor will I in any degree leave you helpless], *nor will I forsake or let you down or relax My hold on you* [assuredly not]!   (Hebrews 13:5 AMP)

Three times in this version of the verse from Hebrews, God basically says, "I will not." This is a wonderful Scripture to memorize and meditate on. He is emphasizing the fact that He will not leave you helpless. Sometimes we may *feel* forsaken because we want Him to do things *our* way, but when raising our shield of faith, we are telling Him, "I believe You and trust You." You can rely on His Word. Begin to say out loud to yourself often, "I trust You even though I cannot see." When you speak it out loud, its truth fills you with faith.

Here is a loaded question: Does your faith in God allow you to believe that His Word will do what it says? It is a question that only you can answer for yourself.

PEOPLE WHO SHOWED GREAT AND SMALL FAITH

Here are two familiar stories from Scripture of two different people, one with great faith and one whose faith was small.

THE WOMAN WITH THE ISSUE OF BLOOD (MARK 5:25-34)

This woman had been bleeding for twelve years. She *"had endured much at the hands of many physicians, and had spent all that she had and was not helped at all, but instead had become worse"* (verse 26). She was isolated and alone. She heard that Jesus was coming to her town and said to herself, *"If I just touch His garments, I will get well"* (verse 28). No one knew she was there in the midst of them. She struggled through the pressing crowd. Her faith had her at a place where she believed she didn't need Jesus to touch her or speak words to her. She only needed to touch His clothing and experience His healing power. As people were pushing up against Jesus, she reached out to touch the hem of His garment.

What a visual scene of faith! The Bible says, *"Immediately the flow of her blood was dried up; and she felt in her body that she was healed of her disease"* (verse 29). Also immediately, Jesus knew that someone had touched his clothing because He felt God's healing power go out of Him. (See verse 30). He asked His disciples who touched Him and they cited the pressing crowd.

> *But the woman, fearing and trembling, aware of what had happened to her, came and fell down before Him and told Him the whole truth. And He said to her, "Daughter, your faith has made you well; go in peace and be cured of your disease."* (Mark 5:33–34)

NO MATTER HOW THINGS LOOK OR FEEL, GOD IS MAKING A WAY WHERE THERE SEEMS TO BE NO WAY. HOLD ON UNTIL HE COMES WITH A TOUCH OF HIS HAND.

After all the years of being sick, when everything she tried for healing didn't work, and after suffering in isolation from others, through the lonely days that dragged into years, when she heard that Jesus was in town, her faith said that if she could just touch the hem of His garment, healing would be hers. Just as this woman experienced, sometimes our shield of faith is tested over many years. We don't know why; we can't figure it out. We question if we did something wrong. We get frustrated and don't understand. And many give up. I suspect she had all of these questions as well. But somehow, without even recognizing it, her faith was growing and she held on until He came. That is the same with us. God's not done writing your story. He cares about you and every aspect of your life. No matter how things look or feel, He is making a way where there seems to be no way. Hold on until He comes with a touch of His hand.

ABRAHAM, SARAH, AND YEARS OF WAITING (GENESIS 15-18)

Their roller-coaster faith is a picture of so many of us in the body of Christ. Starting in the fifteenth chapter of Genesis, Abram asked God why he has no offspring. At first, Abram assumed that maybe Eliezer, who was born in his home, was his heir. God reassured him that *"one who will come from your own body shall be your heir"* (Genesis 15:4). How often do we assume God is going to do something one way because we don't see His plan or His perspective? How many times do we say, "I thought God was going to…?" Abram believed that he would never have children from his own body. His wife Sarai was barren. His perspective was totally different from God's. Taking him outside, God said, *"Now look toward the heavens and count the stars, if you are able to count them.…So shall your descendants be"* (verse 5). From that one seed, his descendants would outnumber the grains of sand and the stars in the sky. Little did Abram know that it was going to be twenty-five more years until that promise came to life through the birth of Isaac.

Read that again…twenty-five years. That is a long time to wait for a promise to come to life. The passage of time can cause your faith to wane. It can cause you to doubt what God has said. It can cause you to walk away from the Lord, or just quit on what you were believing for. Again, when we lose hope, we lose faith, and *"Hope deferred makes the heart sick"* (Proverbs 13:12).

As this story in Genesis continues, ten years have passed since God told Abram he would have an heir. Sarai did not want to wait any longer. She accused God of preventing her from having children and asked Abram to sleep with her maidservant Hagar so that she may have a child through her.

TAKING MATTERS INTO OUR OWN HANDS

Sarai took matters into her own hands. She was going to fix this. It was taking too long; God must have forgotten or He just didn't care. Surely He didn't mean for them to wait this long; she was getting too old. This child would be hers even if it came from Hagar. Isn't it funny how we think we can bully God into our plans? We make our plans and then ask God to fit into them and bless them. I know I have done that a million times, and I'm sure you can say the same thing for your own life. We stop walking by faith and begin to drop its protective shield as fiery darts of time, discouragement, doubt, and unbelief come at us from all angles. Therefore we try to *fix* things, taking control of God's plan, out of His hands into our own. We all know that doesn't work very well for any of us.

Once Ishmael was conceived, dissention rose in Abram's house because Hagar now despised Sarai. The very thing Sarai thought she could step in and fix in her own situation turned against her. So Sarai started to treat Hagar harshly, causing the servant to flee into the wilderness, only to return when an angel told her to do so. Wouldn't you love to be a fly on the wall of this home? Dysfunction and deception on all fronts! This can happen to any of us when we try to control our situation because God is taking way too long. There is a great saying, "Delay does not mean denial." When God doesn't answer our prayers right away and we look around to see what others have and how God has answered *their* prayers, our faith falters. God didn't call us to compare ourselves to others. My pastor always says, "When you compare, you lose."

On the thought of comparisons, another story comes to mind. After He had risen from the dead, Jesus talked to Peter about the kind of death he would encounter, and Peter wanted to know what would happen to John. (See John 21:21.) There was Peter, doing what every one of us does when we look around at the lives of our friends, family, or coworkers, wondering what good thing God has in store for them. Our faith in God begins to diminish. Jesus told Peter, *"If I want him to remain until I come, what is that to you? You follow me!"* (verse 22). Yikes! But that was a great answer because it goes right to the bigger picture; Jesus was asking Peter to follow Him not be concerned with John's mission on earth. Are we not the same? We need to stop looking at someone else's life or social media. Jesus tells us, "What's that to you? *You* follow Me!" Raise your shield of faith over your life and believe God!

GOD DELIVERS ON HIS PROMISE

Getting back to the story of Abram and Sarai, when Hagar's son Ishmael was thirteen, God appeared to Abram again and again promised him a son. He also renamed him Abraham and called his wife Sarah.

> *Then Abraham fell on his face and laughed, and said in his heart, "Will a child be born to a man a hundred years old? And will Sarah, who is ninety years old, give birth to a child?"...But God said,..."Your wife Sarah will bear you a son...at this season next year."*
>
> (Genesis 17:17, 19–21)

So much time had passed that Abraham still did not believe that this child that God had promised him would come from Sarah's womb! He even laughed in his heart. You know God heard that laugh. Abraham still did not have faith to believe what God had promised.

 **WHEN GOD SAYS HE WILL DO SOMETHING, WE CAN BE ASSURED HE WILL DELIVER ON HIS PROMISES.**

When God says He will do something, we can be assured He will deliver on His promises. He is not pulling our chain or trying to make life miserable for us. Even though Abraham was still doubting, God was still going to give him a son. God is faithful and He had a plan and a covenant for Abraham from the beginning. Abraham and Sarah were going to fulfill it, no matter what. That speaks volumes to all of us as well. Even in times of great heartache, pain, and loss, take God up on His promises; take Him at His Word and believe Him.

> *"You are My witnesses," declares the* LORD, *"and My servant whom I have chosen, so that you may know and believe Me and understand that I am He."*
> (Isaiah 43:10)

When Sarah overheard the Lord tell Abraham that she would have a son:

> *Sarah laughed to herself, saying, "After I have become old, am I to have pleasure, my lord being old also?" But the* LORD *said to Abraham, "Why did Sarah laugh, saying, 'Shall I actually give birth to a child, when I am so old?' Is anything too difficult for the* LORD? *At the appointed time I will return to you, at this time next year, and Sarah will have a son." Sarah denied it, however, saying, "I did not laugh"; for she was afraid. And He said, "No, but you did laugh."* (Genesis 18:12–15)

Oh, my goodness, this whole thing is loaded with so many great insights. Sarah laughs just as Abraham did. Obviously their age was a huge factor to them; they could not fathom that they could conceive a child. But God once again has the best line in the middle of all of this doubt: *"Is anything too difficult for the* LORD?" (verse 14).

There it is, my friend. Nothing is too difficult for Him! His plan was set in place and nothing was going to thwart it. That's reassuring for us as well. God did not need perfect or huge faith from Abraham and Sarah to deliver His plan. He had His plan on course, and even though they interfered, He still had a timeframe for what He was going to accomplish. That should truly make you feel secure in your walk of faith. God allows situations to strengthen and grow our faith so we will mature and become more like His Son. Take your shield of faith and stand it up against the fiery darts coming at you. The enemy is a liar. God has not failed you. Hold that shield with confidence, speaking the Word over your situation, and watch God work.

Keep hold of your faith, no matter how small it is, and protect your heart from Satan's darts. Remain standing. Believe that from the impossible, you can see a miracle. The Lord never stops working over the situations in our lives. He has a way of causing all things to work together for good. He is a good, good Father. Hold up that shield and believe Him.

Do you see in these two stories how the shield of faith was being challenged and fulfilled in both circumstances? It doesn't matter what we face; each of us has our own challenges that are personally meant to build a faith that will allow us to stand in the seasons of our lives. This walk of faith is not for the faint of heart. It is for those who have drawn the line in the sand and who will not back down even when they cannot see God answering their prayers.

A FRIEND'S FAITH STORY

I want to share a personal story about my friend Nikki, whose two daughters were both diagnosed with cancer as teenagers. So many watched Nikki dig her feet in, trust God through all her tears and fear, and find a faith above the circumstances. Here is part of the story she wrote:

> The night I left my daughter with her dad in an intensive care unit, I had to drive home and get her belongings as she was about to embark on a journey she never chose for herself. That night I said a prayer from the deepest part of my heart…I told God that no matter what the outcome was going to be, I would still be a servant in His kingdom, even if I lost my child. That night I put my stake in the ground and promised I would never lose my faith even if *victory* wasn't the kind of victory I hoped for.
>
> Life on this earth is fragile, and we ultimately have no control. The true reality I want to share with you that brought me peace and hope during my darkest days was the faith and peace I had in Jesus. It was a peace that held my hand as I drifted into the deep, dark waters of a storm that swirled over my home for three long years. Only through my faith in Jesus Christ have I had the strength to close my eyes and take one step in front of the other. Through my prayers, which were mostly tears running down my face, I experienced such joy that came each morning. The Lord was meeting me every step of the way as I surrendered my

daughter to His care day by day, moment by moment. I never expected this storm to enter our home, but through it, my faith in Jesus has become enriched in standing on His Word. Sometimes I think to myself looking around at so much unsettledness in the world and in our lives...Where is our faith? Where is our hope? Where is our trust? Is it in this mortal material world that offers nothing but uncertainty? Or is it in an eternal God who offers us a free gift through faith and hope in the death and resurrection of Jesus Christ?

Her words are very powerful. As I watched this season of Nikki's life from a distance, I experienced the gospel in full view as I saw her reaction to such a trying, heart-wrenching time in her life. Everyone looking on was inspired and strengthened by her faith. As she said, it was in surrendering to God's will that her faith rose to the challenge, even through the tears. Both of Nikki's daughters are now cancer-free and in their college years of life!

We don't all have our prayers answered exactly the way Nikki has or the way we are hoping. Some of our answers are on the other side of heaven. Our faith cries out and holds onto our trust that God is in the midst of every situation and every detail of our lives. There comes a time in our walk with Jesus that we need to surrender to His perfect will and know that He knows everything about us from the number of hairs on our heads to His thoughts toward us that outnumber the grains of sand. It is a faith He is building in all of us that can stand the test of time. I believe God is building up faith in His people. It will become an immovable faith so that we can withstand the hour we are living in and bring many others to Christ in these difficult times.

If you are challenged in your faith because you have not seen the answer to a prayer, take heart; you are not alone. I encourage you to reach out and grab the hem of His garment. He cares. You were His before time began. You never leave His sight; His eye is always on you. *"We live by faith, not by sight"* (2 Corinthians 5:7 NIV). Hold up your shield and allow your faith to believe even if you cannot see.

A FINAL THOUGHT

 **THE ENEMY OF YOUR SOUL SEEKS TO WEARY YOUR HEART AND SHATTER YOUR SHIELD OF FAITH.**

Your faith is the enemy's biggest target. That's why it is so important to trust God and not come into agreement with the tormenting fiery darts of the enemy of your soul, who seeks to weary your heart and shatter your shield of faith. We cannot place conditions on our faith and trust in the Lord. We can't insist that He has to answer our prayers the way *we* want and on *our* schedule. How silly is that! Let's allow our faith to be unconditional and let us say, "I trust in the lordship of Jesus Christ over my life and even though I don't understand how this situation will work out, I am going to believe You. Nothing can stand against the power of God." He has the final say in our lives. He is at work. I have seen it over and over again both in my life and in the lives of countless others. Hold onto His promises until He comes with His answer.

Speak His Word over your life, sing worship songs out loud to the Lord, and thank Him for His blessings. Hold up that shield of faith with confidence. Without even you noticing it, your faith is growing!

TAKE ACTION

When you stand up, putting on the armor of God for this fourth piece, with your arm bent, like you are holding a shield in front of you, *say out loud*, "The shield of faith. With respect to the promises of God, I shall not waiver in unbelief but shall stand firm. For whatever God has promised, He is able also to perform."

WARFARE PRAYER

Lord, I ask that You will help me to believe when I cannot see, to trust Your character as You are working all things out for my good. I thank You that You see every detail of my life and have not forgotten where I am. Thank You that I only need a tiny bit of faith for You to move mountains and restore my life. Lord, help me as I hold this shield of faith in front of me. The enemy loves to throw fiery darts to steal my hope and trust in You. Thank You for providing me with Your shield of faith so that every one of those fiery arrows from the enemy is extinguished by Your Word that I speak forth from my mouth. Thank you for constantly leading me to a path of true faith in You, a faith to stand the test of time. Nothing can come against the power of my God. I raise my shield of faith and stand with the Captain of the hosts of heaven. In Jesus's name, amen.

SIX

YOUR MIND...
IT'S A TERRIBLE THING TO WASTE

And take the helmet of salvation.
—Ephesians 6:17

DON THE HELMET OF SALVATION

When a soldier readies for battle, the helmet is the last piece of armor to go on. It is vital for survival. If you suffer major head injuries, the rest of your armor will be of little use.

The assurance of our salvation is our defense against anything the enemy throws at us, and this knowledge must be in our minds at all times. Because of the power of the cross, our enemy no longer has any hold on us. He knows that, but he is banking on the fact that most of God's children do not know or understand that truth completely. So he exploits their ignorance and takes advantage of it.

Over the years, I have enjoyed watching many football games. I have never seen a football player go on the field without a helmet. They know that their helmet has been made specifically to protect their head and their brain from terrible injury, either from being hit by an opposing player or from hitting their head on the ground. In the same way—even more so—we cannot walk out of the house without our helmet of salvation to protect our thoughts and our minds from the tactics of the enemy. There is a great battle for your mind, and you need to know how to fight it in the Spirit.

Buckle on that helmet. It helps you fight against every imagination, every stronghold, to take captive every thought that is against the knowledge of God. A stronghold is any thought that holds you captive, or builds a thought process that's difficult to break. God has given us a sound mind. You don't have to wrestle this out without His help. He stands in your defense, *"That you be renewed in the spirit of your minds"* (Ephesians 4:23).

THE DEVIL WANTS YOU TO PAY ATTENTION TO YOUR FEELINGS, WHICH ARE FICKLE, FLEETING, AND OFTEN BASED ON FALSE ASSUMPTIONS.

The slogan, "A mind is a terrible thing to waste" speaks the truth. The enemy loves to mess with your mind and your way of thinking, bringing suggestions that are laced with lies and deception. The devil wants you to pay attention to your feelings, which are fickle, fleeting, and often based on false assumptions. Jesus wants you to pay attention to His truth, which is unchanging and cannot deceive.

The battlefield of the mind is real. It is imperative that we use the Word of God and our knowledge of His salvation against negative thoughts to take them captive. The Lord is quite aware that we all battle thoughts that simply are not true but sound factual or trustworthy.

You must learn to use the Word of God against the assault on your thinking. As you wear the helmet of salvation every day, your mind becomes more insulated against the suggestions, imaginations, schemes, desires, and traps the enemy lays out for you. It is our choice to take those thoughts captive and guard our mind and our heart in Christ Jesus. (See Philippians 4:7.)

DO NOT WAR IN THE FLESH

The first thing that we must understand about this helmet is that it is designed to protect our minds from negative thinking. Many of us become trapped by detrimental thoughts that steal our peace, hope, faith, and whatever other good thing God has placed within our hearts to enjoy life. Let this Scripture help in this area of the flesh:

Though we walk in the flesh, we do not war according to the flesh. For the weapons of our warfare are not carnal but mighty in God for pulling down strongholds.

(2 Corinthians 10:3–4 NKJV)

Though we are flesh, we are never to war according to our flesh. We will lose that battle every time. The flesh and the spirit are always going to be at war with each other. *"For the desire of the flesh is against the Spirit, and the Spirit against the flesh; for these are in opposition to one another, in order to keep you from doing whatever you want"* (Galatians 5:17). What a war that is within us! The desires of our flesh are against the Spirit. The flesh, with its emptiness, wants to be satisfied, but refuses the idea of satisfying it by the Spirit. *"Because the mind set on the flesh is hostile toward God; for it does not subject itself to the law of God, for it is not even able to do so"* (Romans 8:7).

That's why it helps to be aware when the flesh is rising up within, causing us to react in opposition to God's Word. We are to war in the Spirit, where we pull down those strongholds in our lives programmed by our past and our experiences. We are getting hit in our flesh and our minds by flying shrapnel that the enemy throws at us on a daily basis. Remember, things aren't always as they seem. We have the authority, in God's Word, to walk in the Spirit so that we will not carry out the desires of the flesh. We need our spirit man to grow stronger than our flesh.

DESTROY THOSE THOUGHTS

> *We are destroying sophisticated arguments and every exalted and proud thing that sets itself up against the* [true] *knowledge of God, and we are taking every thought and purpose captive to the obedience of Christ.*
> (2 Corinthians 10:5 AMP)

Look at what this verse is saying. We are to destroy *every* imagination, speculation, and lofty thing that's raised up against the knowledge of God. *This is our answer!* How many times have you and I been captured by the imagination or speculation of a situation in our lives that was not real, yet we played it over and over in our minds like some never-ending movie? We did not take that thought captive to the obedience of Christ. We just went with it, failing to heed the knowledge that salvation is ours through Jesus! We did not consider first what the Lord has to say about the situation by turning to His Word.

If the Word of God is living and active, sharper than any two-edged sword (see Hebrews 4:12), then we need to be serious about using it to fight against the battle of our mind. We all have to deal with what comes in and goes out of our minds on a daily basis. If we don't know what to do with those thoughts, we can find ourselves in a stronghold of anger, offense, condemnation, and every other thing Satan will choose to throw at us because we let those thoughts run wild. I have personal experience with this.

Years ago, God challenged me to take my thoughts captive by using His Word over a certain area of my life. Using index cards, I wrote down about five Scriptures relating to that stronghold over my mind. I spoke those Scriptures over myself in my devotions every morning and took the cards with me wherever I went. I recited them in my car, at the grocery store, and at the mall! I was saying them over and over throughout the day. It got to the point that I had memorized them and was letting the truth of those Scriptures wash over me.

WHEN THE STRONGHOLD AGAINST ME BROKE, I WAS SHOCKED AT THE FREEDOM I WAS EXPERIENCING.

After two months of doing this daily, the stronghold broke. It didn't happen right away; it did take some time. If you spend twenty minutes to dwell on the wrong thoughts, it will take more than twenty minutes to be rid of them. It is like taking a sledgehammer to a brick wall. It won't make a dent on the first swing; it may not even break a single brick. You have to keep swinging until it falls. When the stronghold against me broke, I was shocked at the freedom I was experiencing. I saw plainly that the Word of God is absolutely alive and powerful. I know that it will break any stronghold in *your* life. It is a truth I stand on. When we submit to God first, the enemy must flee.

"Is My word not like fire?" declares the LORD, *"and like a hammer which shatters a rock?"*   (Jeremiah 23:29)

Putting on the helmet of salvation takes great commitment and time. Unfortunately, too many of us don't take the time to put the Word in our hearts and minds like this, so we stay numb in our thinking and the enemy's onslaughts grow bolder. It's time to change that!

JESUS IN THE WILDERNESS

I am reminded of what Jesus did in the wilderness when Satan was throwing tempting thoughts at Him, trying to cause the sinless Son of God to sin. (See Matthew 4:1–11.) Have *you* ever fasted for forty days and forty nights? I never have, but I have had friends who have fasted that long, although not as completely as Jesus. They have told me that their fasts were challenging but the spiritual rewards were overwhelming.

After fasting in the wilderness for forty days and forty nights, Jesus was understandably very hungry. So what temptation do you think Satan comes at Jesus with first? Food! Do you see his schemes? Do you see how he hits you when you are at your weakest? Jesus was hungry and Satan tried to plant a thought into His head about turning the stones into bread. I'm sure in His exhaustion and hunger, Jesus could picture bread in His mind. But because of His relationship to His Father, and knowing not to bow to Satan's schemes, He quotes the Word back to the enemy: *"It is written, 'Man shall not live by bread alone, but by every word that comes from the mouth of God'"* (verse 4 ESV). If the enemy will try to lie, twist, and deceive Jesus with the Word, he will certainly do it to us as well. And he has been trying to do so since the garden of Eden.

BUCKLE THAT HELMET

So let's see how we can use the helmet of salvation effectively. It must be buckled tightly to protect our minds daily. Our enemy is not playing games; he's deadly serious about trying to hold us captive with harmful thoughts. We must focus on renewing our mind with God's Word.

> *And do not be conformed to this world, but be transformed by the **renewing of your mind**, so that you may prove what the will of God is, that which is good and acceptable and perfect.*   (Romans 12:2)

To help you renew your mind, I suggest getting a pack of three-by-five-inch index cards. Obviously, you will not be using all of these at once, but as circumstances change in your life, the Scriptures for you to stand on will change. I highly recommend that you teach this to your family and friends, your spouse, your children, your nieces and nephews—everyone near and dear to your heart. I have a massive stack of index cards. I don't tell you that to brag, but to share how much I depend on God's Word.

Let's say you are praying for freedom from a sin habit or a mindset, either for yourself or for someone you love. Do you realize that we can pray for someone on the other side of the world, and it is heard, received, and acted upon by the power of the Holy Spirit? There is no distance in the Spirit. Thank God for that!

To counter a sin habit or mindset, here are just three Scriptures that you could write down on three separate index cards and begin to speak them out loud over your life. Make the Scriptures personal by using *me* or *I* where it may say *us, we,* or *you*. If I was speaking these over my life, this is how I would say them:

[I] *trusted and committed* [myself] *to the* LORD, *let Him save* [me]. *Let Him rescue* [me], *because He delights in* [me].   (Psalm 22:8 AMP)

When you commit yourself, that habit, or that sin to the Lord, look at the payback: He will deliver and rescue you. Why? Because He delights in you! Read that again. He delights in you! He is not disappointed in you. There is never a day when the Lord looks at you and thinks, "This child of Mine has ruined everything." He is not mad *at* you; He is mad *about* you. Oh, my friend, know how much you are loved and cherished by your King. He delivers, rescues, and delights in you!

*If [I] confess [my] sins, He is faithful and righteous, so
that He will forgive [my] sins and cleanse [me] from all
unrighteousness.*   (1 John 1:9)

If we confess our sins. There is a condition on God's
forgiveness. We need to confess and repent first. The Lord
doesn't put a requirement of what kind of sin it is. He doesn't
care. Jesus already paid the cost of that sin on the cross. But
we have to do our part by confessing and bringing it before
Him. Sin has no weight when you are blameless before Him.
How I love this Scripture! It is very freeing and quite powerful to grasp His love and forgiveness.

*Throw off your old sinful nature and your former way of
life, which is corrupted by lust and deception. Instead, let
the Spirit renew your thoughts and attitudes. Put on your
new nature, created to be like God—truly righteous and
holy.*   (Ephesians 4:22–24 NLT)

Take off that old way of thinking, that old sin. You are a
new creature in Christ. That old man is dead. Do you hear
that? Your old man is dead when you come to salvation in
Jesus. Our job is to put on the new self of redemption and
restoration created in the likeness of God. Take off the old;
put on the new.

Can you see, with just those few examples, how to use
the Word to battle the overflow of negative and condemning thinking and self-talk? No one can do this for you. You
must stand in the battle for your mind and speak the Word of

God over yourself. Your victory will be sure, but you must put on that helmet of salvation. You will be amazed by the peace and freedom you will encounter as the Word works on your behalf. Our thoughts, emotions, and feelings are controlled by the mind. We must have proper programming from the Word of God to have clear victory over our lives.

A FINAL THOUGHT

Please understand how much God loves you and how much His thoughts are toward you—not the thoughts that condemn, but the thoughts that bring life.

God spoke to my heart years ago about the way I was talking so negatively to myself about myself. The Lord insisted that I study Psalm 139 and start believing His thoughts toward me. I ended up memorizing the entire psalm.

> *How precious also are Your thoughts for me, God! How vast is the sum of them! Were I to count them, they would outnumber the sand. When I awake, I am still with You.* (Psalm 139:17–18)

His thoughts toward us outnumber the grains of sand. Have you ever gone to the beach, picked up a handful of sand, and tried to count the grains in your hand? I didn't think so. It would be impossible. There are too many in just a handful, let alone the entire beach! That is how much God thinks about you and me—it is limitless. Can we even fathom that? He endlessly thinks about you. You are never out of His view. He doesn't want us speaking negatively about ourselves because He's certainly not doing that.

These days, when any negative thoughts pop up in my head, I know where they are coming from and I know what to do with them. It has taken a ton of work, but the negative way I talk to myself about myself has diminished tremendously.

 **ANY NEGATIVE THOUGHT THAT COMES TO YOU IS NOT GOD SPEAKING TO YOU, SO TAKE IT CAPTIVE AND SPEAK HIS WORD INSTEAD.**

Remember, any negative thought that comes to you is not God speaking to you. He talks to you in a very loving, positive way. So when those negative thoughts start to form, you can take them captive, knowing that is not your God talking to you. It is either how you programmed yourself to think, or the enemy trying to deceive you. When you understand that and use God's Word over your life, I'm telling you, you are going to see a great victory in your life!

I have practiced using the Word of God on index cards for many, many years. The Word is deeply embedded in my heart and spirit. I have come such a long way with the battle of my mind. Remember, the battle is a daily thing. I don't stay on a subject for weeks or months anymore. The battle is no longer a movie. It may last a few days or a week at times, but I immediately know where it is coming from and get right back under the shadow of the Most High.

*He who dwells in the secret place of the Most High shall
abide under the shadow of the Almighty. I will say of the
LORD, "He is my refuge and my fortress; my God, in
Him I will trust."* (Psalm 91:1–2 NKJV)

You can have the same thing. The more the Word of God
comes alive to you, the more you won't want to go back to
feeling depressed and defeated. You will walk in victory for
the battle belongs to the Lord. He will take what the enemy
meant for evil and turn it for good.

It takes time and discipline to reprogram your mind and
protect it from Satan. Don't give in to the fight; don't let the
enemy run wild in your mind. Take the time to get free. You
have the helmet of salvation, which is your armor against his
voice. Put it securely on your head. Use it and walk in peace.

*Finally, brothers and sisters, whatever is true, whatever is
honorable, whatever is right, whatever is pure, whatever
is lovely, whatever is commendable, if there is any excel-
lence and if anything worthy of praise, think about these
things.* (Philippians 4:8)

Stand firmly, for indeed, your mind is a terrible thing to
waste!

TAKE ACTION

When you stand up, putting on the armor of God for this
fifth piece, put your hands on your head as if you were putting on a helmet, and *say out loud*, "The helmet of salvation.

Though I walk in the flesh I do not war according to the flesh. For the weapons of my warfare are not of the flesh, but they are powerful before God for the pulling down of strongholds. I am destroying imaginations, speculations and every lofty thing raised up against the knowledge of God. And I am taking every thought captive to the obedience of Christ."

WARFARE PRAYER

Jesus, I buckle this helmet of my salvation tightly on my head. I thank You that as I have confessed with my mouth and believed in my heart that You rose from the dead and that You alone are the Savior of the world, my salvation is in You and You alone. And I thank You that as I battle the enemy for what goes in and out of my mind on a daily basis, I will recognize his accusing words to me knowing they are not coming from You, dear God, but from Satan, who can only fight by deceiving and intimidating with lies. I thank You, Lord, for giving me the power through Your word that is a weapon of my warfare to combat this vile accuser. He has nothing on me as I dwell under the shadow of Your wings and fight back with the words from Your Scripture that make him cower. Lord, You promised that no weapon formed against me would prosper. I thank You that as I speak Your Word, the enemy must flee. I buckle this helmet daily and watch Your thoughts become my thoughts and Your ways become my ways as we walk this journey together in strength and power. In Jesus's name, amen.

SEVEN

HIS LIVING WORD

And the sword of the Spirit, which is the word of God.
—Ephesians 6:17

CARRY THE SWORD OF THE SPIRIT:
THE LIVING WORD OF GOD

Roman soldiers carried a short sword known as a gladius, which was designed for close-quarters combat. The lethal blade was sharpened on both sides, so that it sliced and cut no matter how it was wielded. The sword is the only offensive weapon in the armor of God.

USE THE WORD

> *For the word of God is living and active, and sharper than any two-edged sword, even penetrating as far as the division of soul and spirit, of both joints and marrow, and able to judge the thoughts and intentions of the heart.*
>
> (Hebrews 4:12)

I hope you have noticed that everything I refer to you for victory in your life is in the Word of God. The Bible says it is *"living and active, and sharper than any two-edged sword."* It brings you answers to life's challenges, glory to God's name, cuts through the darkest thoughts and makes you whole, cleanses the stench of sin as far as the east is from the west, and judges the thoughts and intentions of the heart. It is one of the most potent tools you need to combat the enemy's tactics over your life. That is why it is the only offensive weapon used in this armor.

USING GOD'S ALIVE AND ACTIVE WORD SETS YOU FREE AND MAKES THE ENEMY SHUDDER!

IT'S LIVING AND ACTIVE

The Word of God is alive because Jesus is alive and He is the Word. (See John 1:1.) The Word is God-breathed. When God breathed and spoke over the earth, it came alive. When you speak His Word over your situation, it comes alive and it becomes active over your life. The enemy is afraid of the Word because he knows it works. He knows it has power to destroy him and his plans. He lies so much to you and me because he knows the Word is true. He wants you to think the Word is boring or irrelevant, especially in today's culture. The truth is, God's Word is powerful; it works and the devil knows it. It sets you free as it reveals his tormenting tactics. When we believe in God, and we trust and believe His Word, it makes the enemy shudder. *"You believe that there is one God. Good! Even the demons believe that—and shudder"* (James 2:19 NIV). Stand on this verse. Using God's Word, which is alive and active, sets you free and makes the enemy shudder!

SHARPER THAN ANY TWO-EDGED SWORD

Have you ever seen a two-edged sword in action? I have. A colleague of mine demonstrated how lethal it can be, holding the sword in one hand and a letter-sized piece of paper in the other. He wielded that sword in every direction and cut that paper to shreds. Everyone was amazed at how easily that sword cut. Yet, the Word of God is even sharper, cutting thoroughly and deeply. It cuts through every doubt, every discouragement, every heartache, every fear, every condemnation, and every ugly thing the enemy can think of. God's Word cuts through it all. It does not come back empty either. It waters our lives with hope, love, faith, joy, assurance, and peace.

As the rain and the snow come down from heaven, and do not return to it without watering the earth and making it bud and flourish, so that it yields seed for the sower and bread for the eater, so is my word that goes out from my mouth: it will not return to me empty, but will accomplish what I desire and achieve the purpose for which I sent it.   (Isaiah 55:10–11)

The Word will accomplish and succeed in what it promises!

ABLE TO JUDGE THOUGHTS AND INTENTIONS OF THE HEART

The Word is so cutting and powerful that it will show us when our thoughts or intentions are wrong. Why? Because God loves us and always wants the best for us. He wants us on the right course He has planned for our lives. So often, we don't even know our own heart, but He does. And His Word will show us the real intentions of our hearts, good or bad.

ALL SCRIPTURE IS GOD-BREATHED

All Scripture is God-breathed and is useful for teaching, rebuking, correcting and training in righteousness, so that the servant of God may be thoroughly equipped for every good work.   (2 Timothy 3:16–17)

It's not enough to memorize or mediate on Scripture; you must believe that it is inspired, that it literally is breathing God's wisdom over your life.

Let's make this a solid and clear statement: *all* Scripture—not some verses, not a few chapters, but all of it—is inspired by God. It is not just a book of stories written only by men, as some would believe. God inspired those men as they were writing. He breathes life over His Word. That's why it has such longevity in our lives. It is not progressive with the times or the culture. Don't be fooled by the world's standards as they try to change the Bible to fit their narrative. His Word never changes. If it did, it would be a false religion. Jesus is the Word. That's why you can stake your life on its truths. *"In the beginning was the Word, and the Word was with God, and the Word was God. He was in the beginning with God"* (John 1:1–2).

The Bible is profitable for teaching, reproof, correction, and training in righteous. It teaches us how to live a life of truth, wisdom, hope, freedom, and love, how to treat our neighbor, how to train and discipline our children, what to do when we are angry, and everything else we need to know in order to live a life that is pleasing to God.

FOR REPROOF AND CORRECTION

He disciplines us for our good, so that we may share His holiness. For the moment, all discipline seems not to be pleasant, but painful; yet to those who have been trained by it, afterward it yields the peaceful fruit of righteousness. (Hebrews 12:10–11)

God disciplines us; He does not punish us. There is a huge difference. Discipline is training someone to obey rules or adhere to a certain behavior, whereas punishment is severe, rough, suffering treatment. God disciplines us when the need arises because He loves us and wants us to become better people. He is not punishing us.

FOR TRAINING IN RIGHTEOUSNESS

We are all in a growing process under the loving, attentive, very detailed eye of God. He trains us in right living. With so much moral decay in our society, where the truth is suppressed and we are told things like, "If it feels good do it," "There are no absolutes," "Abortion is not murder," "Gender is a social construct," and "There is no moral compass," God's Word speaks loud and clear. *"Be diligent to present yourself approved to God as a worker who does not need to be ashamed, accurately handling the word of truth"* (2 Timothy 2:15).

As the enemy tries to trap us in circumstances, situations, and mindsets, we have a two-edged sword that we can wield to combat those lies and deceptions: the truth of God's Word. Standing on it takes work. We must spend time daily with the Lord in prayer, worship, and Bible reading. This is a relationship with God; it's more than a religion, so it takes time, commitment, and discipline to walk by faith and come into His presence. He longs to spend time with you. Set a time and a place you will go to meet with Him every day. Jesus often did this Himself. *"In the early morning, while it was still dark, Jesus got up, left the house, and went away to a secluded place, and prayed there for a time"* (Mark 1:35).

THE LORD IS WAITING FOR YOU. DON'T LET THE ENEMY MESS WITH YOUR WALK IN THE LORD!

The Lord is waiting for you. If we skip this part, our life of faith will be weak because we have not picked up the sword of the Spirit, the living Word of God, as often as we should. One of my favorite books about prayer is *The Hour That Changes the World* by Dick Eastman.[9] It challenged me to set this time aside daily and experience the presence and power of God, building an intimate relationship between us. Don't let the enemy mess with your walk in the Lord!

A FINAL THOUGHT

IF you put this into practice and use His Word like the two-edged sword that it is, you will live a life of great victory! A perfect life? No. Will you have all the answers you want in a timeframe of your choosing and in your own way? No. But you will have the most powerful tool in your hand to defeat the enemy of your soul. You will not be a victim of Satan's schemes; you will become his greatest nightmare! Satan fears the power of God's Word. As a child of the Most High, watch and see what God's Word will do in any challenge.

9. Dick Eastman, *The Hour That Changes the World: A Practical Plan for Personal Prayer* (Grand Rapids, MI: Chosen Books, 1978).

He is a good Father. He can take all circumstances or decisions and redirect them on a dime as we pray and stand on His Word. He sees the road twisting and turning through our lives, and He wants to direct those steps as we let Him. *"Your word is a lamp to my feet and a light to my path"* (Psalm 119:105). Spending time with the only One who has the directions to His heavenly kingdom is the greatest blessing in our lives. You and I are so valued in His eyes that this walk with Him is worth fighting for. Raise and wield that sword!

> *One who pays attention to the word will find good, and blessed is one who trusts in the* LORD. (Proverbs 16:20)

TAKE ACTION

When you stand up, putting on the armor of God for this sixth piece, put your right arm up in the air like you are holding a sword in your hand and *say out loud*, "The sword of the spirit, which is the living Word of God. Greater is He that is in me than He that is in the world. No weapon formed against me shall prosper. The Word of God is living and active and sharper than any two-edged sword."

WARFARE PRAYER

Heavenly King, I draw my sword of Your Word that is capable of cutting through every circumstance and situation in my life. It is alive. It is always active. You have taught me that as I wield my sword with

Your words of truth, the battle belongs to You. The
enemy is afraid of Your Word because he knows that
it works. You used it against him many times in the
Bible and have taught me to do the same. I see how
the enemy tries to twist your Word in this culture to
make it relevant to his lies. With confidence in You, I
lift up my sword that breaks through the darkness in
and around me. Thank You for drawing life and light
back into my spirit and heart as I hold steady in Your
Word. You are the only true God. You are the first
and You are the last, and beside You there is no other
God. I stand firm with the high praises of God in my
mouth and a two-edged sword in my hand. In Jesus's
name, amen.

FINAL CHARGE

THE BATTLE IS REAL...
THE VICTORY IS SURE

The high praises of God shall be in their mouths,
and a two-edged sword in their hands.
—Psalm 149:6

When we walk in faith and courage, we are free! I trust this study ministered to you and will be empowering as you walk out your faith in Jesus Christ. Instead of guns and tanks, we have learned to fight with God's armor. It has been made quite clear to us that this battle is real. The enemy wants territory—and that territory is you, your family, and your friends. But we are smarter now, and we know how to fight!

Don't open that door to Satan's voice anymore; when you hear it, turn the tables on him and lift up the powerful name of Jesus. A pastor once said, "The enemy wouldn't tie you up if he wasn't afraid of what would happen if you got loose!" Satan is afraid of Christ within you; he knows the Lord's light will dispel his darkness. Put on that full armor and worship God!

SATAN IS AFRAID OF CHRIST WITHIN YOU; HE KNOWS THE LORD'S LIGHT WILL DISPEL HIS DARKNESS.

The Lord will lead and direct your life in amazing ways as you trust Him. He is as close to you as you want Him to be. We serve a very faithful God who keeps His promises through the seasons of our lives. Every promise from the Scriptures is God's written letter to us. In understanding that, we can say to God while in prayer, "Thank You, Lord, for doing as You promised."

Please don't be misled; God is still on His throne. He is not nervously pacing heaven over our situations or our world. He has everything completely under control. Satan is a mouse with a megaphone. He sounds louder at times, but in reality, he squeaks while running away when we speak the Word back at him. Use what you have been taught.

The Lord wants to bring revival back to our hearts. Revival means dead things come to life. Come to life, my friend! Arise to a new life in Christ and live. Put this on an index card on your bathroom mirror:

Arise [from spiritual depression to a new life], shine [be radiant with the glory and brilliance of the Lord]; for your light has come, and the glory and brilliance of the LORD has risen upon you. (Isaiah 60:1 AMP)

Jesus, through the power of the Holy Spirit, is so incredibly aware of you that as you continue to reach for His hand in times when you are weary, He will fill you with strength from on high. He will change your situation, accomplish things at the perfect time, move the mountain in your heart and life, and restore the years that have been stolen. Jesus will do all of this for you because you are loved and you are His. All the fire we go through is refining us.

Fire tests the purity of silver and gold, but the LORD tests the heart. (Proverbs 17:3 NLT)

YOU DON'T HAVE TO BE PERFECT FOR GOD TO LOVE YOU.

You are so unconditionally loved that you don't have to perform for Him. You don't even have to be perfect for Him to love you. Your sins don't even keep Him away; that's when He embraces you the most. He is proud of you; He is smiling at you; and He brags about you to the Father. Your name is registered in heaven. Your life on earth is His gift to you. He wants you to enjoy it. He has offered you an abundant life, so embrace it. You are the apple of His eye and He loves you with an everlasting love.

Put on the armor of God and stand with your King!

You did not choose Me but I chose you, and appointed you that you would go and bear fruit, and that your fruit would remain.   (John 15:16)

THE ARMOR OF GOD WITH SCRIPTURE REFERENCES

GIRD MY LOINS WITH THE GOSPEL OF TRUTH

Jesus is the way, the truth, and the life. No one comes to the Father but by Him. (See John 14:6.)

THE BREASTPLATE OF RIGHTEOUSNESS

I am in right standing before God because of what Jesus has done for me. (See 2 Corinthians 5:21.)

SHOD MY FEET WITH THE GOSPEL OF PEACE

Peace I leave with you, My peace I give to you. Not as the world gives do I give to you. Let not your heart be troubled nor let it be fearful. (See John 14:27.)

THE SHIELD OF FAITH

With respect to the promises of God, I shall not waiver in unbelief, but stand firm. For whatever He has promised, He is able also to perform. (See Romans 4:20–21.)

THE HELMET OF SALVATION

Though I walk in the flesh, I do not war according to the flesh. For the weapons of my warfare are not of the flesh but they are powerful before God for the pulling down of strongholds. I am destroying imaginations, speculations, and every lofty thing raised up against the knowledge of God. And I am taking every thought captive to the obedience of Christ. (See 2 Corinthians 10:3–5.)

THE SWORD OF THE SPIRIT, WHICH IS THE LIVING WORD OF GOD

Greater is He that is in me than he that is in the world. (See 1 John 4:4.)

No weapon formed against me shall prosper. (See Isaiah 54:17.)

"The word of God is living and active, and sharper than any two-edged sword" (Hebrews 4:12).

ABOUT THE AUTHOR

Luanne Botta is an author, Bible teacher, and speaker who brings the gospel to life through the Word and personal testimony. Her high energy and joyful, encouraging spirit carry an authentic transparency, making her an endearing and powerful speaker.

As a high school teacher at a private Christian academy for almost twenty years, Luanne found herself in a unique role, guiding hundreds of young people through God's Word with her uncompromising, take-no-prisoners way of speaking the truth while still showing them unconditional love. Her passion was igniting them to live their lives with a higher standard than the culture around them.

Aided by those years of teaching, Luanne authored two books to equip high school teens on the godly truth of sexual integrity and character: *Young Hearts. Pure Lives* (for girls), and *The Warrior Within* (for guys). She challenges teens to raise the standard in their lives and stand firm against the culture around them that is spinning out of control.

Luanne has brought her passion to women's ministry as well. She has over fifteen years of experience teaching the Word of God and facilitating women's Bible studies. She is a sought-after speaker for women's events and retreats. She recently recorded a podcast with Moms In Prayer International about *Spiritual Warfare and the Armor of God: The Battle Is Real...The Victory Is Sure*. She prays that this book conveys the vital importance of spiritual warfare for all audiences—men and women, teens and adults, individuals, church groups, and Bible studies.

Together with her friend Mary Ann Crum, Luanne also cohosts a weekly podcast entitled *Unquenchable Hope* on the Spodify, Apple, and Google podcast networks. It encourages women to trust in the hope they have in Jesus as they go through life's challenges.

Luanne is available for seminars, retreats, chapels, and conferences for women, teenagers, young adults, and parents, with an anointing and passion to share the gospel of Jesus Christ. Throughout her years of ministry, Luanne's greatest joy has been "to bring a voice of encouragement and hope to those who are looking for truth...and to walk humbly with my God."

For additional resources or to contact Luanne, visit:
www.luannebotta.com

Welcome to Our House!

We Have a Special Gift for You

It is our privilege and pleasure to share in your love of Christian books. We are committed to bringing you authors and books that feed, challenge, and enrich your faith.

To show our appreciation, we invite you to sign up to receive a specially selected **Reader Appreciation Gift**, with our compliments. Just go to the Web address at the bottom of this page.

God bless you as you seek a deeper walk with Him!

WE HAVE A GIFT FOR YOU. VISIT:

whpub.me/nonfictionthx

WHITAKER
HOUSE